THE COMMONWEALTH AND INTERNATIONAL LIBRARY

Joint Chairmen of the Honorary Editorial Advisory Board

SIR ROBERT ROBINSON, O.M., F.R.S., LONDON

DEAN ATHELSTAN SPILHAUS, MINNESOTA

Publisher: ROBERT MAXWELL, M.C. M.P.

The Kibbutz

A NEW WAY OF LIFE

Frontispiece. Statue of Mordechai Anielevitch, Commander of the Warsaw Ghetto Revolt, in Kibbutz Yad Mordechai. In the background, water-tower shelled during the War of Independence. (David Perlmutter [Kfar Menachem].)

The Kibbutz

A NEW WAY OF LIFE

BY

DAN LEON

WITH A FOREWORD BY

ANTHONY WEDGEWOOD BENN, M.P.

THE QUEEN'S AWARD
TO INDUSTRY 1966

PERGAMON PRESS

OXFORD · LONDON · EDINBURGH · NEW YORK
TORONTO · SYDNEY · PARIS · BRAUNSCHWEIG

Pergamon Press Ltd., Headington Hill Hall, Oxford
4 & 5 Fitzroy Square, London W.1

Pergamon Press (Scotland) Ltd., 2 & 3 Teviot Place, Edinburgh 1

Pergamon Press Inc., Maxwell House, Fairview Park, Elmsford,
New York 10523

Pergamon of Canada Ltd., 207 Queen's Quay West, Toronto 1

Pergamon Press (Aust.) Pty. Ltd., 19a Boundary Street,
Rushcutters Bay, N.S.W. 2011, Australia

Pergamon Press S.A.R.L., 24 rue des Écoles, Paris 5ᵉ

Vieweg & Sohn GmbH, Burgplatz 1, Braunschweig

Copyright © 1969 Dan Leon

Israel Edition *The Kibbutz—A Portrait from Within*, published by

"Israel Horizons" 1964

This edition revised and enlarged 1969

Reprinted 1969

Library of Congress Catalog Card No. 69–12386

Printed in Great Britain by A. Wheaton & Co., Exeter

08 013356 8 (flexicover)
08 013357 6 (hard cover)

Contents

Preface

THIS book sets out to provide an introduction to the Kibbutz Artzi Hashomer Hatzair, the largest of the four national federations of kibbutzim (communal settlements) in Israel. Since it is written by one of its members, it does not pretend to be "neutral" in the sense that, like the writings of some outside observers, it can view the kibbutz coldly and dispassionately from the vantage-point of a comfortable seat in the stalls. It is written from the inside, by one who is totally involved in, and concerned about its struggles, its achievements and its problems. It was C. Wright Mills who wrote at the beginning of one of his books: "Throughout I have tried to be objective, but I do not claim to be detached."

Whether this is an advantage or a disadvantage, the reader must judge for himself. In the author's opinion, the "scientific" observations of observers studying the kibbutz from outside are not infrequently distorted and lacking in understanding, because their preconceived notions make it hard for them to sense the dynamics of kibbutz life, the revolutionary nature of which challenges so many assumptions taken for granted elsewhere.

For my part, I have tried to present the kibbutz as I know it and live it, and to avoid the pitfalls of propagandists who project the kibbutz and Israel as an idyll, photographed in glorious technicolour. The book presents the problems, as well as the achievements, in the conviction that those who gloss over the harsh dilemmas of kibbutz life and the kibbutz future do it poor service, however worthy their intentions.

Since this is a portrait of, and from within, the Kibbutz Artzi, when I refer to the kibbutz in this book, as a rule I refer to the Kibbutz Artzi and do not pretend to speak in the name of the other kibbutz movements. Yet it is important to bear in mind that whatever differences there may be between the federations, and between

vii

kibbutzim of the same federation, all kibbutzim and all kibbutz members are far more united in their way of life by what they have in common than they are divided by their differences, real and important as they are. With all the variations, the theme is common to all.

It follows that much of what is written here about the Kibbutz Artzi is also true of other kibbutzim. Except when it seemed important to explain the particular approach of the Kibbutz Artzi to a very few questions of special significance, I considered it was outside the scope of this work to deal in detail with the differences in approach to kibbutz life between the various movements. In so far as I deemed it essential to touch upon political problems, the views expressed here are those of Mapam, with which the Kibbutz Artzi is affiliated. Again, as a member of Mapam, the author does not claim to be "objective" in the sense of non-involvement.

It must be pointed out that although this edition was completed in 1968, it does not deal with any of the complicated and controversial problems relating to the areas occupied by Israel during the Six-Day War of 1967. To do justice to these matters, which at the time of writing are far from an agreed solution, would have meant including much political material which, vitally important as it is to the future of Israel in all its aspects, I considered to be outside the scope of a book about the kibbutz as such. Therefore, all comments on Israeli territory and settlement refer to the position before June 1967.

Though in general the views expressed here are those of the Kibbutz Artzi, they are formulated at the author's own responsibility. Broadly speaking, it may be assumed that they are generally representative of those of the whole movement. This book has drawn freely and unreservedly from books and articles written by kibbutz members, very often without specific acknowledgement, for it is the accumulation of innumerable individual opinions which together constitutes what one may call "kibbutz public opinion".

I would like to express my thanks to all those kibbutz members without whose advice and assistance this book could never have appeared. On a more personal note, I would conclude by remarking that it would be presumptuous to dedicate such a modest book to anyone, but if it were to be dedicated it would be dedicated to my own kibbutz, Yasur, which is both my home and the source of my own kibbutz experience and inspiration.

Kibbutz Yasur,   DAN LEON
   Western Galilee, Israel,
      1968

Foreword to the Israeli Edition

IN 1945 four of us—all R.A.F. pilots stationed in Egypt—wrote off to the Jewish Agency in Jerusalem and asked if they could arrange for us to spend our leave at a kibbutz in Palestine. In response to this request we were invited to Shaar Hagolan near the Sea of Galilee where we were most warmly welcomed and had a wonderful opportunity to see the work of the settlement and to meet those who lived in it. But the most memorable event of all could not have been anticipated. For it was actually while we were there that Hitler's Germany surrendered. That evening the whole kibbutz commemorated the event with speeches and a bonfire and we all danced with joy half through the night. There can have been few families there who had not been personally bereaved as a direct result of the nightmare from which we were emerging. But the emphasis was all on the future and especially on the resettlement and socialist reconstruction to which they had set their hands. So strong was this positive spirit that we, who had for years been trained and conditioned to kill and destroy the enemy, were completely caught up in the mood of peaceful co-operation which characterised the occasion.

I have followed the progress of my friends at Shaar Hagolan ever since, revisiting it twice more: once, in 1956 when the Fedayeen raids were at their height, and again in 1963 to observe its astonishing development. Each time I have been there and to the other settlements of the Kibbutz Artzi I have been impressed by the same spirit of these dedicated socialist Jewish communities practising successful voluntarism and developing new values of lasting importance. Since then, I have always wanted to know more about the history, organisation, development and future of the Hashomer Hatzair Kibbutzim. Dan Leon's excellent and detailed book exactly meets that need and will, I'm sure, interest the general reader as much as it will those who live and work within the traditions of the movement that he describes.

He tells us about the story from its very beginning and about the role of the kibbutzim in reuniting a people in dispersion with the land of Israel—not just in a geographical but in a physical, agricultural and spiritual sense too. "When the strong hand of the Jewish peasant once more guides the plough the Jewish problem will be solved." How many people hearing those words of Herzl can really have imagined that such an aspiration could actually be realised. And yet can anyone who has seen a kibbutz member tilling the soil and living so fully within a collective, doubt the truth of that prediction? The sad, persecuted, petit bourgeois Jew of the Diaspora has been transformed by his contact with the land.

But this is not just another colonial settlement that has been established. This is no land *élite* living off the labour of native workers like the settlers in South Africa or the colons in Algeria. The socialist inspiration of Hashomer Hatzair has been built upon the dignity of personal labour and the elimination of class-exploitation. In the hard desert areas where the Kibbutzim began their pioneering there was grass roots socialist democracy at work even before the first cultivable crop came up for the harvest. It is so easy for a visitor to talk enthusiastically about these achievements and overlook the appalling problems that confronted the pioneers, both in earlier years and in the new settlements today, which still operate under siege conditions.

The book also deals very fully with the production problems that confront any kibbutz and the painfully slow process of capital accumulation. It deals with the internal structure which has been built up for reaching decisions not only on the productive side but also on the distributive side as well. And there can be quite as many difficulties in deciding how you allocate the surplus as in planning how to achieve it! The problems of human identification between the individual and the community within a total collective are of intense and special interest to the man or woman from the outside. We soon learn that it is not the rigid discipline, poverty and obedience of a monastic order that we are studying but a happy, outgoing, successful human organism founded on new principles. For the sociologist, it is the kibbutz as a new society that holds the greatest interest. What is the role of the family within a total collective? How are the educational experiments succeeding and what have they got to offer the wider community? Will the cultural vitality of the early settlers survive against the commercial pressures of modern society?

Many of these questions have already been answered by the younger generation themselves—the boys and girls of the kibbutz who have settled down naturally and unselfconsciously in the pattern of life which their fathers and grandfathers made for them with their hearts and minds and hands. The young pioneer settlements in the Negev desert show that those who were brought up with these new values have not settled back to take them for granted but are competing amongst themselves to exceed the achievements of those who went before. The importance of the kibbutz today lies in the fact that it offers an effective, practical, dedicated and successful alternative focus of life to those which nurtured within the affluence of any modern state, including the State of Israel. This competition between the two ideals of society, between a socialist agricultural collectivism and a capitalist urban individualism provides one of the most interesting and creative tensions in Israel today.

For those who come from the underdeveloped areas of the world to study what is being done in Israel there is no doubt that the kibbutz movement holds the greatest interest. It is far more relevant to the problems of pioneering and leadership that they face at home than is the bright life of Tel Aviv. And they can identify more closely with the non-racial socialist ideology of the Kibbutz than with any other group of Zionists. Perhaps, too, it is on this sort of basis that Jew and Arab can find their common destiny within a united and peaceful Middle East—freed from exploitation and nourished in unity by the soil in which both communities have such deep roots.

It may well be that the relevance of the Kibbutz movement is of even wider importance than that. People all over the world are moving towards a socialist form of society, by many paths. It would be surprising if those who are trying to evolve an organic structure for the societies which they aim to create did not find much to inspire and help them in the experience of the collective settlements which are described so fully in this book.

London, 1 May 1964   ANTHONY WEDGWOOD BENN

PART 1

FOUNDATIONS

The Kibbutz Movement, in spite of its limitations and difficulties, is the biggest and most successful "utopian" revolutionary experiment that has been attempted and the closest approach to the way of living at which Communism aims. . . . The Kibbutzim are nowadays Israel's most effective contribution to the millenary messianic promise of justice and peace; and this contribution is in a large measure due to unbelievers inflamed by the same ardour that consumed Isaiah.

GEORGES FRIEDMANN, *The End of the Jewish People?*

THROUGH nearly 2000 years of Dispersion, during which the stormy waves of history carried the Jewish people through continents and regimes spanning the broadest horizons of human experience, the links binding the people of Israel to the Land of Israel were never broken. The rebirth of Israel as an independent state in 1948 can only be understood as a chapter in the story of a people shaped by history and shaping history. The harsh reality of Jewish life in Dispersion, and the historical will of the Jewish people to rebuild its national life and to restore its ancient glory in Eretz Yisrael* (Palestine) are among the themes dominating this long and epic story, in which human tragedy and courage are written so large.

Modern Zionism, the national liberation movement of the Jewish people, dates back to the last decades of the nineteenth century. When its first pioneers reached Palestine, they found a Jewish population of less than 25,000, most of whom lived in poverty and degradation. Yet by 1965, two and a quarter million Jews lived in Israel, of whom a million and a quarter immigrated since the Declaration of Independence in 1948.

This transformation has been widely described as "miraculous". But historical miracles are wrought by men of flesh and blood dreaming and hoping, planning and struggling, living and dying for the realisation of their personal, national and social aspirations within the context of their times. The early pioneers would sing a Hebrew song which starts with the words, "We have come to the Land to build it and to be rebuilt by it." And the history of Israel's pioneers, in which the kibbutz has played a vanguard role for over fifty years, is a human miracle only in so far as it is a saga of courage, devotion and tenacity without which neither the land nor the people of Israel could have been reborn.

For a twofold historical challenge faced those whose efforts paved the way for the regeneration of the Jewish people in Israel.

* *Eretz Yisrael*: Hebrew for the Land of Israel, Palestine.

3

They found a land suffering from centuries of neglect and stagnation: her once fertile plains and hills and valleys, estimated in ancient times to have been an important agricultural centre for a primarily Jewish population of some two and a half million, provided only a most primitive livelihood for the current population of about half a million Palestine Arabs. They found, too, a small Jewish community living on charity from abroad, pious and poverty-stricken, awaiting the coming of the Messiah in suffering and humiliation.

The task of the pioneers was to transform *both the physical and the human landscape* of Palestine, to redeem both the land and the people. Before and after the First World War this was the mission of Israel's early pioneers—young Eastern European Jews, themselves the sons of a people long divorced from the soil, from agriculture and from physical labour.

HERZL AND WEIZMANN

Theodor Herzl (1860–1904), the founder of modern political Zionism and the convenor of the first Zionist Congress at Basle, Switzerland, in 1896, noted in his diary: "If I were to sum up the Congress in a word—which I shall take care not to publish—it would be this: at Basle, I founded the Jewish State. If I said this out loud today, I should be greeted by universal laughter. In five years, perhaps, and certainly in fifty, everyone will perceive it." Herzl's prognosis was, of course, astoundingly correct, as the State was founded in 1948, fifty-one years after the Congress.

It was the same Herzl who told the doubtful and faint-hearted among his followers: "*If you will it, it is no dream.*" Chaim Weizmann (1874–1952), who led the Zionist Movement through the critical decades of upbuilding and struggle between two world wars and lived to become the first president of the State of Israel, called his volume of memoirs, *Trial and Error*.

In these two phrases—"If you will it, it is no dream", and "trial and error"—can be found the threads running through the history of Israel's rebirth and binding together all those pioneering endeavours which started at the end of the last century, gathered momentum during the turbulent period of the October Revolution (1917) and the Balfour Declaration,* and progressed, unevenly yet steadily in the 1920's and 1930's until they culminated in the struggle against British rule, the War of Liberation of 1948 and the current decades of Jewish sovereignty in Israel.

In these concepts, we can find, too, the motive-forces behind the birth and development of the kibbutz movement, from Degania, the first of Israel's communal settlements, which was established in 1910. Like those which followed, *it was not constructed from a blueprint* worked out in advance. The will and the dream were in evidence from the start, but the process of trial and error regulated the form and content, and the pioneers who laid the foundations could not know how the edifice would have to grow and change, constantly adapting itself to face the new challenges thrown up by changing circumstances.

NATION AND HOMELAND

In other words, the development of the kibbutz movement must be seen as an integral part of the broad national and social struggles which accompany every national liberation movement through the different stages of the long road to freedom. Far from developing in a void, the birth and subsequent growth of the kibbutz were dictated by the special demands of the Jewish movement for self-emancipation. This is the key not only to a correct understanding of the past history of the kibbutz movement, but also to a correct evaluation of its current perspectives, to which we shall return in our concluding chapter.

The kibbutz movement has grown over fifty years from the handful of pioneers who settled in 1909 on the banks of the Sea of Galilee (Lake Kinneret) and founded Kvutsat† Degania in 1910,

* Issued by the British Government in 1917, recognising the Jewish National Home in Palestine.

† Though there was originally a slightly different meaning to the Hebrew words *Kvutza* and *Kibbutz*—communal settlement—they are virtually identical today.

to a great network of some 225 communal settlements with a total population of over 90,000 men, women and children in the 1960's. During the same period, the Jewish population of Palestine has grown, as we have seen, from some 25,000 to over 2,000,000. This historical process, known as the "Ingathering of the Exiles", is a dominant factor in twentieth-century Jewish history.

Since the destruction of the Second Temple by the Romans in the year A.D. 70 and the suppression soon after of the Bar-Kochba revolt, we are dealing increasingly and eventually almost exclusively, with an *extra-territorial people*—a people denied of a land, and therefore an *abnormal people*. It is the history of a people drenched in the blood of generations of martyrs, and including the unparalleled tragedy of the massacre of six million Jews by Nazi Germany.

Centuries of persecution moulded the national character of the Jewish people while they wandered through the paths of the Dispersion, driven from place to place by historical forces over which they had little control, suffering, creating and adapting themselves to new continents and social regimes. The changing reality of this broad and varied historical canvas, with its many dimensions of time and place, of economic, social, political and cultural changes, has left its mark on the Jewish people, just as the history of every people can only be understood within the dynamic context of change and struggle, action and reaction.

By the end of the last century, the Jewish masses in Europe were caught up in the throes of a turmoil which undermined the very foundations of their life. In Czarist Russia they were the victims of the harshest discrimination and persecution, so that between 1881 and 1914 alone, over three and a half million Jews emigrated from pogrom-ridden Europe, of whom only 2 per cent went to Palestine.

The uniqueness of this, the most persecuted people in the world, had various foundations. First, the Jews were geographically dispersed as unwanted minority groups among other peoples. Second, they stood out as an alien element clinging to their own religious, cultural and social forms. But in addition, history had imposed upon their national life a completely abnormal economic structure.

THE JEWISH ANOMALY

Here were a people lacking any connection with the soil, with agriculture and with nature, divorced from the primary means of production both rural and urban. Tolerated as long as the host nations were in need of the intermediary economic functions which the Jews performed in trade and commerce, in those liberal professions which suffered them, and in secondary working-class occupations like tailoring, they were the natural scapegoats in periods of instability and upheaval. This, the economic uniqueness and vulnerability of the Jews in Dispersion (expressed, of course, in different forms according to changing historical circumstances) was always, and remains today, at the root of the Jewish problem everywhere.

Lacking the possibility as well as the desire to assimilate because of their uniqueness, the Jewish masses were at best enabled to transfer the Jewish problem from place to place, but never to solve it. The only radical and permanent solution lay in the territorial concentration of this scattered people, yet this, too, would be a will-o'-the-wisp unless accompanied by a social transformation no less radical and revolutionary than the actual act of geographical concentration. The normalisation and stabilisation of Jewish life demanded, in addition, a return to the land, to agriculture and to physical labour. This was the only outlet which offered a prospect of tackling the Jewish anomaly at its roots.

The future was to show that in their wanderings in a contracting world, the Jewish minorities in many parts of the globe would increasingly be brought face-to-face with the harsh realisation that they were unwanted everywhere and had nowhere to turn except to their own national homeland. The Nazi holocaust in Europe, when six million Jews, one-third of the whole people, were physically annihilated, was the terrible result of the failure to learn this lesson in time.

THE ROOTS OF THE KIBBUTZ

This, the catastrophic consequence of Jewish history in Dispersion, was, of course, unknown to the first pioneering waves of

Zionist immigrants who made their way to Palestine. Their sense of history taught them three basic lessons. They must settle in Israel rather than perpetuate the Dispersion. They must return to the soil and to productive labour. The new society which they would build as workers and pioneers in their own land must be founded on the progressive social principles expressed in various streams of socialist thought which had influenced them profoundly in their countries of origin.

We have already noted that the first tiny kibbutz groups approached the building of their settlements without a blueprint to guide them. The kibbutz was an answer to the hostile wastelands awaiting redemption by Jewish labour, and to the social aspirations of the settlers. All former attempts at Jewish colonisation through the classical capitalist method of private ownership and wage labour had failed. The first wave of Zionist pioneers who had come to Palestine with high hopes at the end of the nineteenth century had been forced to give up the struggle, degenerating into employers of cheap Arab labour or vassals of Jewish philanthropists abroad.

We have touched upon some of the influences which motivated the foundation of the first kibbutz groups, and they would certainly include the following:

⋆ The supreme test of settlement, colonization and physical security could best be tackled by the joint effort of a group united by common aims, and fortifying the will and staying-power of the individual through complete mutual aid and responsibility.

⋆ This would facilitate the transition to agricultural labour of young people unaccustomed to its rigours, especially in the harsh and primitive conditions of the new land.

⋆ It would make possible the absorption and integration into the new life of new settlers from future waves of immigration.

⋆ The group would be founded on the individual consciousness of every settler, and the whole framework would be entirely voluntary, lacking any form of external coercion.

⋆ It would be based exclusively on self-labour by Jewish

workers, and they would undertake every type of work, however hard, including the guarding of their own security.

* The group would be democratically self-governed, and completely equalitarian. Equal rights would be granted to all, and there would be full equality for all in everything. This would include equality between men and women, between original settlers and newcomers, and between all members regardless of the work performed.

* The kibbutz would play a pioneering role not only in settlement, but also in shaping the image of the new socialistic society in the Jewish homeland.

The kibbutz form of settlement, as it developed before and after the First World War, was therefore founded on the idea of Jewish farmers working nationally owned land through the collective ownership by the whole group of all the means of production— soil, equipment, livestock, etc. The group would share whatever profits were made according to the principle of "from each according to his ability, to each according to his needs" (within the economic possibilities of the commune). In other words, the kibbutz was conceived as a communal, as against a private or co-operative settlement, in which all members would share equal responsibilities and receive equal compensation. There would be no class division between employer and employees; those responsible for running the farm would be democratically elected, but would enjoy no special privileges; all decisions on the economic and social life of the commune would be made by the members themselves.

DIFFERENT STREAMS WITHIN THE KIBBUTZ MOVEMENT

Within this—largely unwritten—set of guiding principles, the first kibbutz groups, numbering ten to twenty members each, grappled with the manifold economic and social problems facing them at every stage of their development. In fact, some fifteen years separate the foundation of Degania from that of a federation of similarly-minded kibbutzim, which is today known as *Ichud Hakvutzot Vehakibbutzim* and was associated with the Mapai party.

The other two major kibbutz federations, the *Kibbutz Meuchad*, associated with the Achdut Avoda party, and the *Kibbutz Artzi Hashomer Hatzair*, associated with the Mapam party, were both founded in 1927. These three federations, all of which are a part of the Israel Federation of Labour, the Histadrut, today account for some 96 per cent of kibbutzim. The remainder of the kibbutzim are either religious or nonaffiliated settlements.

Outside observers sometimes find it hard to understand this diversification within the kibbutz movement, and ask why it is necessary. A careful reading of the foundation programme of the Kibbutz Artzi (which we shall call, for the sake of brevity, the K.A.), dated 1927, can indicate the answer. For it deals with two matters: the functions of the kibbutz as an instrument for the realisation of the national and social aspirations of the Jewish people; and the kibbutz as a new society, envisaged as "the prototype of the future socialist society" in Israel.

The crystallisation of three main federations of kibbutzim can be seen as the inevitable result of varying approaches to both matters. It must also be borne in mind that as the early kibbutz groupings sought to consolidate and expand their first struggling points of settlement, they naturally made contact with similar-thinking groups of pioneering Zionist youth abroad who offered the obvious source of future reserves.

GROWING PAINS

It is not our task to examine in detail either the stages of consolidation, or the different conceptions which were ultimately to characterise each federation. However, in retrospect it would seem that the development of different streams was one of the factors which enabled the kibbutz idea to attract different types of immigrant youth and to secure more reserves from Zionist youth movements abroad. Though united on the basic idea of communal settlement in Israel, these movements expressed quite varied political and social philosophies and drew their inspiration from different ideological and spiritual sources, both general and Jewish.

There were, for example, those who believed in a very small, intimate, family-like kibbutz unit, of which Degania was the first and which influenced a part of the present-day *Ichud*. On the other hand, the *Kibbutz Meuchad* saw the need for large communes open to all. In the early 1920's, its precursors even founded a "labour battalion" (*G'dud Ha'avoda*) which they envisaged (boldly though wrongly) could develop into a general nation-wide commune of all Israel's Jewish workers, who numbered only a few thousand in those days. The Kibbutz Artzi took up a position between the two extremes—the "organic kibbutz" which would grow systematically, constantly absorbing new age-groups into the fabric of its communal life.

Of course, some of the questions which looked so vital to the first pioneers appear less so in the 1960's, when there are three generations in the kibbutz. As regards the size of kibbutzim, the Kibbutz Meuchad has a very few large settlements with a population of about 1500 but these are the exceptions rather than the rule. The average size of the kibbutzim in the three Federations was about the same in the early 1960's—380 in the Kibbutz Meuchad, 361 in the Kibbutz Artzi and 326 in the Ichud. (Details of the K.A. population are to be found in the statistical appendix.) Significantly, the variations in size of kibbutzim within the different groupings are larger than those between them. In the 1920's, however, the developments of the future could not be known or foreseen. There was no example to follow, no blueprint to copy. The only guidelines were the ideals and aspirations of the settlers and the only framework for their realisation—the incredibly tough conditions of a backward and undeveloped Palestine.

The settlers were exposed to frightful physical dangers in the early years, facing the pains of acclimatisation to back-breaking agricultural labour in the unaccustomed climate and landscape of the new country. Only a burning faith, sense of mission and creative imagination could envisage how to effect the transformation of the tiny camp of tents, housing a handful of barefooted pioneers in a malaria-ridden and hostile environment, into the flourishing settlements with hundreds of members and children which we take for granted today.

On some important internal problems, there are still diverse opinions in the different federations. These are often thrashed out in inter-movement forums, for every kibbutz member would agree that on many basic questions of kibbutz living much is common to all the kibbutzim. We shall refer briefly to some of these questions when we discuss the actual workings of the kibbutz.

However, we must emphasise that the internal social fabric of the kibbutz, the way in which it educates its children, the rights and obligations of members, the integration of new generations—all these cannot be divorced from another problem (or more correctly, series of problems) which can be defined as the role and tasks of the kibbutz in the national and social struggle of the Jewish people and of the new Israel. Here, the Kibbutz Artzi Hashomer Hatzair developed its own unique approach.

THE KIBBUTZ ARTZI PLATFORM

The distinguishing feature of the K.A.'s world-outlook (as laid out in the 1927 programme) is that it is founded on a synthesis between pioneering Zionism and revolutionary Socialism, between construction and social struggle. Correctly envisaging that the territorial concentration of the Jewish people in Israel is a deep-rooted historical process dictated by the conditions of Jewish life in Dispersion, it rejects as Utopian the idea that territorial concentration can be effected without regard to the development within Jewish society of social differentiation and class struggle. Since private capital will in the main be attracted by the lure of quick and easy profits, the workers themselves must take the lead in the establishment of a self-supporting Jewish economic base, concentrating on pioneering agricultural colonisation and the development of basic industry.

While private capital and initiative will be welcome as long as they lend their weight to constructive upbuilding, the capacity to absorb a growing Jewish population will depend primarily on national capital and self-governing workers' enterprises. Only in this way can the abnormal Jewish economic structure be normalised and the Jewish masses productivised.

The special and unique conditions in which the uprooted Jewish people is returning to a backward and pioneering country demands, therefore, not only the actual creation from scratch of a Jewish peasantry and working-class: they themselves must also undertake the major burden of colonisation and construction. Failing this, they will have no "strategic base" for the realisation either of their national or their social aspirations.

While the ultimate goal is the realisation in Israel of a fully socialist society, the K.A. renounces as an illusion the idea that this can be achieved overnight. During the first stage, it will be necessary to maintain a degree of inter-class co-operation within the Zionist movement for the attainment of common goals. These include the winning of national independence, the strengthening of the productive base and the absorption of mass immigration. Without this, all talk of Zionist and socialist realisation alike degenerate into empty phraseology.

Through its hegemony in the process of Zionist realisation, the young Jewish working class must build up its own strength, guarding its own class interests, its independence and its militant ideology at every stage. In fact, in the words of Ber Borochov (1880–1917), the most outstanding Socialist–Zionist theoretician, "Zionism will be realised through class struggle, or it will not be realised at all".

It should also be pointed out that already in 1927, the K.A. defined its Zionist and Socialist orientation most clearly. In the Zionist movement it saw "the expression of all those forces within the Jewish people united for the upbuilding of the country (Israel) and for the national renaissance; the workers' movement in Israel is an organic part of the working-class movement in the world, struggling for the liberation of the working-people and the abolition of classes". At the same time, it adopted a forthright internationalist attitude towards the Arab question, rejecting the domination of one people by the other and stressing its conviction that Jewish–

Arab relations must be founded on equal rights, co-operation and international solidarity between the progressive forces within both peoples.

THE ROLE OF THE KIBBUTZ

What is the role of the kibbutz within this all-embracing political conception? The 1927 programme states that "the K.A., as a part of the kibbutz movement, sees in the kibbutz:

(a) the pioneering cells of a new society,
(b) a constructive and colonisatory instrument of the Jewish working class,
(c) an instrument for the absorption of productive Jewish immigration,
(d) a base for the class struggle.

"Every kibbutz in the K.A. is an organic unit. The kibbutz is not only a class or national weapon, for it is also an independent way of life—the prototype of the future socialistic society, and an ideological collective."

This exposition of the essence of the Hashomer Hatzair kibbutz, though written many years ago, can hardly be bettered today. It makes clear above all that the kibbutz is at one and the same time an *instrument* of Socialist–Zionist realisation and *an independent way of life* in itself. In so far as it is both an instrument and an end in itself, so to speak, it puts into daily practice those values of self-labour, productive work, equality, democracy and mutual aid which, most highly developed in the commune, are of significance for all the Socialist–Zionist forces and for the whole of Israel.

The kibbutz internal structure and way of life are the surest guarantees that its members will be activised not only within the commune for its own internal aims, but that through the commune they will play a pioneering role in the upbuilding both of the land and of the conscious working class growing with the land. As such, the kibbutz is the highest expression of the synthesis between pioneering construction (Zionism) and class struggle (Socialism).

One of the tragedies of the kibbutz movement is that the K.A. was the only one of the three major federations which understood , from the outset that because of the kibbutz's dual nature as a political tool or instrument, as well as an independent way of life—it must be united as a political, as well as an economic and social, collective. Indeed, this concept was bitterly attacked for years.

The experience of all the federations was to show that without internal political unity, the kibbutz lacks one of the dimensions without which it cannot function effectively. Unfortunately, this lesson was only learned at the expense of a bitter split along political lines in the Kibbutz Meuchad federation in 1951. This involved the break-up of long-established kibbutzim, population transfers and even family rifts. From its inception, the K.A. has crystallised its own unified political concepts through the same democratic processes by which it determines all its policies, economic, social, educational, etc., and each kibbutz is a branch of the Mapam party.

THE YEARS OF DECISION

Though we have noted that the historical and spiritual sources which nourished the kibbutz movement in its early stages were not without certain traces of Utopianism, there can be little doubt that the rapid development of all the major kibbutz streams can only be explained in terms of the pioneering role which the kibbutzim played in the upbuilding and defence of Jewish Palestine before the creation of the State of Israel in 1948. The Israel commune would have gone the way of other communal experiments within a capitalist society (nearly all of which can be said to have failed to face the challenges of modern society because of their Utopian character) were it not for the fact that far from cutting themselves off from the main stream of current Jewish history, the kibbutzim played a vanguard role in the Jewish national and social revival in Israel.

This is true not only in the colonisation of the wastelands, in the development of Jewish agriculture and in the defence of Jewish settlements. The kibbutz was also in the forefront of every phase of the struggle for political independence against the reactionary Arab leadership and the forces of British imperialism. Since the kibbutz was the cradle of a new type of Jewish worker, rooted in the land, independent and highly class-conscious, it was natural that the labour movement in Israel should have been decisively influenced in its most formative period by the kibbutz movement. Far and away above its numerical proportions, the kibbutz provided cadres of leadership for the Jewish population in the major political, social and security struggles which culminated in the establishment of the State.

From the beginning, right-wing circles within the Zionist Movement viewed with alarm what they called these dangerous "Communist experiments". A Labour Zionist report dated 1920 stresses that these reactionary circles saw in all the forms of workers' colonisation purely transitional forms of settlement and "had no intention of founding workers' villages. . . . On the contrary, their idea was to sell the property to small private settlers" for "the management of the farms must not be given over to the workers . . . because the communal principle sabotages all initiative." "The enemies of the working-class are loudly proclaiming to the Zionists in Palestine and abroad that self-labour means poverty, the kvutza (kibbutz) bankruptcy, and that only private farming can redeem the situation."

The Labour–Zionist leader, Kaplansky, warned in 1927 that "the attack upon the kibbutz is only the beginning of an all-out attack upon (independent) workers' colonisation, and if successful it will liquidate other 'social illusions' like the *Moshav*"—the small-holders' co-operative settlement, which dates from the year 1920. It is also interesting to note that during the whole of the 1920's, the kibbutzim were not permitted by the Zionist authorities to build permanent buildings unless they would be suited to the needs of family farms and small peasants.

This situation was not changed until the Labour–Zionist factions won a majority in the Zionist Movement in the early 1930's, and the twelve years from 1936 to 1948 saw Zionism and Palestine pass through a series of decisive events: the Arab disturbances of 1936–9, British hostility towards Zionism culminating in the decision to "freeze" Jewish Palestine through the prevention of immigration and settlement, the Second World War (during which Jewish Palestine mobilised itself for the Allied war effort), the open struggle against British rule from 1945, the United Nations decision of 1947 to partition the country between independent Jewish and Arab states linked in an economic union, and the War of Liberation of 1948 which followed the British refusal to co-operate with the U.N. and the invasion by six Arab armies intent upon the physical destruction of Israel.

DEVOTION AND EXAMPLE

These momentous years witnessed the rise of the kibbutz movement, backed by the progressive majority within Zionism, to the pinnacle of its achievements. The borders of settlement were pushed forward and defended by the kibbutzim against Arab attacks and British hostility, the same borders which were defended by the settlers in the heroic and costly struggles of the War of Independence against the Arab invasion armies. A people's army was built, the legendary Palmach (striking-force of the Israel Defence Army), which was constructed, led by and based upon the kibbutzim. Tens of settlements like Negba and Yad Mordechai, Hashomer Hatzair kibbutzim in the South, held back the Arab invasion while the young Israeli army gathered strength enough to hit back and eventually drive out the invaders. In those epic days, it can be simply stated that the kibbutzim saved the young State of Israel from the danger of physical extermination.

Limitations of space do not allow us to dwell upon the role of the kibbutz movement and of its emissaries in other aspects of the struggle for independence, such as the mighty movement of "illegal" immigration from liberated Europe, or the establishment during one day in 1946 of eleven pioneer settlements in the Negev: in every task which called for pioneering initiative and human courage, the kibbutz was ready and able to mobilise its members to organise and carry out the work in hand. Without this devotion and this example, who can say what history might have held in store for the national movement of a small people fighting with its back to the wall against larger and more powerful forces determined upon its destruction?

We are dealing, therefore, not only with a new communal society searching for correct solutions to burning internal problems. What we have before us in the kibbutz is the political vanguard of a people involved in a prolonged endeavour to normalise its national and social life through territorial concentration and the return to the land. At one and the same time, this people must rebuild itself and its homeland and forge the tools of political independence, finally achieved through the toil of its pioneers and the blood of its fighting youth.

Is it any wonder that within these varied campaigns, in field and factory, in the political arena and on the battlefield, there crystallised from the early days of the return to the Land different approaches to the ways and means by which the broad aims of the kibbutz could be fulfilled? It was around the kibbutz movements that the political parties within the labour movement developed, so that in fact—if not in theory—the principle first formulated by the K.A. in 1927 that the kibbutz is an ideological, or political, as well as a social and economic collective, is now practised as far as possible by all the kibbutz federations.*

THE TEST OF TIME

When we return to the position of the kibbutz in the State of Israel, we shall see that this is very closely related to the historical background which we may now sum up. Since the foundation of the K.A. more than forty years have passed. In 1927 it numbered

* In the 1961 elections to the Israel Knesset (Parliament), 93·1 per cent voted Mapai in the Ichud Federation, 86·8 per cent voted Achdut Avoda in the Kibbutz Meuchad, and 98·3 per cent voted Mapam in the Kibbutz Artzi. These figures give a clear enough indication of the extent of political unity in all the federations, even if the register in the kibbutzim often includes small numbers of voters who are not kibbutz members. In 1965, with the split in Mapai, the overall picture remained the same but Ben Gurion's Rafi group won some votes in the Ichud.

250 members in four kibbutz groupings. By 1966 it encompassed seventy-three kibbutzim with a total population of 30,000, more than a third of the whole kibbutz population and the largest of its major streams. Of course, none of these can, or would, claim a monopoly of achievement, for each has made its own special contribution according to its particular historical development and principles.

It would be impossible in our day to envisage the map of Israel without the 230 kibbutzim, half of which have been established since the foundation of the State in 1948, including over thirty of the K.A. These younger settlements, nearly all of which are on or near the 1949 borders fulfil indispensable tasks in the security and development of the areas whose new colonisation they have pioneered.

These seventy-three Hashomer Hatzair settlements represent a great creative force, producing 10·5 per cent of Israel's total agricultural output and developing new industrial branches; they have absorbed many thousands of youth and adults from the new immigration; they are busily engaged in integrating the second generation into kibbutz life; and their educational system is the envy of many progressive educationalists abroad as well as in Israel itself. Furthermore, they are important centres of the new Hebrew culture growing in Israel, and the home of some of the country's foremost creative artists, writers, musicians and folk-dancers. Last, but not least, they form a vital part of the Left-Socialist Mapam, which was one of the three major working-class political parties in independent Israel.

These achievements are not recounted in order to minimise the problems facing the kibbutzim in the 1960's and 1970's, or the role played by the various kibbutz federations in building the movement. But it would seem that it is no exaggeration to state that *the basic principles of the Kibbutz Artzi Hashomer Hatzair have stood the test of time*. It has proved its ability to face the demands of the turbulent decades through which the Jewish people have passed since the founders of the Kibbutz Artzi formulated their unique contribution to Socialist–Zionist theory and practice.

T.K.—B

Perhaps the outstanding reason for this has been the remarkable *unity of theory and practice*, without which the daring vision of the founders could not have been transformed into a living reality. Directed as it has always been, and is today, by the Socialist–Zionist approach to Jewish life and by the general tenets of Marxism,* the Kibbutz Artzi has had no historical parallel to follow in its translation of these principles into the language of a commune fighting for its future within the capitalist society surrounding it.

This demanded a clear understanding, neither dogmatic nor opportunistic, of the social forces at work inside and outside the kibbutz, and of their relation to each other. It meant seeing the kibbutz as a new way of life within the changing social and national character of the society around it, and in the wide world outside it. This sense of historical continuity, which binds together the chain of settlements and the chain of ideas of Hashomer Hatzair, is the secret of its ability to grow and develop with the times, while remaining faithful to the vision of its founders.

CREATING FACTS

On its course within the Labour–Zionist forces, many allies have marched with the Kibbutz Artzi and not a few enemies have crossed

---

* Unfortunately, the Marxist classicists never attained a deep understanding of the motive-forces at work in Jewish life in the Dispersion and of the processes underlying Jewish territorial concentration in Israel.

Marx and Lenin saw the solution of the Jewish problem in assimilation, and denied its national character. Stalin's definition of nationality excludes the possibility of an extraterritorial nation, and he wrote in 1913: "What sort of a Jewish nation is this, made up of Georgian, Dagestanian, Russian, American and other Jews who do not understand each other (speak different languages), live in different parts of the globe, never met each other and will never meet together, neither in peace nor in war?"

Some thirty years later, six million of these Jews understood each other for the last time as they were herded into the Nazi gas-chambers to speak the common language of martyrdom. The destruction of one-third of our people in Europe and the continuing mass immigration to Israel, where the creative impulses and the everyday life of the people are commonly expressed in the Hebrew language—all this has shown the fallacy of the assimilatory approach to the Jewish fate and future.

its path as it progressed from stage to stage over thirty-five years. Its constant loyalty to the synthesis of constructive upbuilding and class struggle, of pioneering Zionism and revolutionary Socialism, has been scorned, attacked and distorted both from the Left and from the Right. So-called Leftists have disowned it from a Socialist point of view because of its constructive Zionist consistency, while the Right has sought out contraditions between its Zionist patriotism and its Socialist convictions.

Consequently, the movement has been compelled to fight a battle on two ideological fronts, as it were. But it was not a campaign conducted primarily with slogans and pamphlets and electioneering, for the Kibbutz Artzi is an ideological collective, but not a political party. As such, its efforts have been concentrated upon merging the actual construction of its own settlements with the search for allies among Socialist–Zionist elements in the Jewish working class, among the Arab masses and in the international labour movement.*

This educational venture has been conducted in the kibbutzim among adults and youth in order to equip them for the myriad tasks involved in the independent functioning of workers' settlements, with their unique economic, social, educational and political ramifications. The same fundamental aim has characterised the educational work of Hashomer Hatzair among the youth and the

---

* The K.A. played a leading role in the formation of the political party called the Socialist League (1936), of the Hashomer Hatzair Workers' Party (1946), and of the United Workers' Party Mapam (1948). All these were composed of the membership of the K.A. and their allies among the working class and the progressive intelligentsia. Mapam, which enjoys the support of nearly 100,000 Jews and Arabs, is the second largest force in the Israel Labour movement (*Histadrut*). It was represented in the 1965 *Knesset* (Parliament) by 8 members (out of 120), 5 of whom are members of Hashomer Hatzair kibbutzim. Altogether, there are 17 members of kibbutzim in the *Knesset*—5 Mapam, 4 Achdut Avodah, 3 Mapai, 2 Rafi, 2 from the religious parties and 1 Liberal (1967). Five members of the Cabinet are from kibbutzim. According to Joseph Ben-David in *Agricultural Planning and the Village Community in Israel* (UNESCO, 1964) in 1960 22 *Knesset* members were past or present members of kibbutzim and another 5 were from the Moshavim. Eight out of 20 Cabinet members were "connected with kibbutz or moshav".

new immigrants in Israel, and among Jewish youth abroad. For the special strength of the movement has been its ability to educate new generations of youth for pioneering, to speak the language of youth, to nurture among youth the national and social values without which the rapid growth of the Kibbutz Artzi could not have been achieved.

Jewish youth, imbued with these values through the educational work of Hashomer Hatzair in Israel and abroad over fifty years, has been, and is today, the life-blood of the movement. This educational work has spread to new continents, carried by the emissaries of the Kibbutz Artzi and inspired by its vision and its example.

PAST AND FUTURE

The kibbutz is an entirely voluntary society, the members of which may apply to join or decide to leave its ranks as they please. It would seem to us that two overriding criteria determine the extent to which the kibbutz stands or falls, grows or stagnates, and is more or less capable of meeting old and new problems, both in its day-to-day life and in its historical tasks:

1. the correctness of its essential premises and the extent to which they answer the challenges both of the building of kibbutz society and its integration into the national and social struggle of the Jewish people (and of people everywhere striving for a better and juster life for themselves and their children);
2. the extent to which these premises, this ideology, can fortify the conviction and faith, the will to work and the personal identification of the kibbutz member—and his sons and grandsons—with the way of life and the tasks of the commune.

Now, this inheritance is gradually passing into the hands of the sons and daughters of the founders, along with thousands of youth from all over the Jewish world who have been inspired by the Kibbutz idea. The theory and practice of the Kibbutz Artzi Hashomer Hatzair have provided the mainspring for pioneering achievements second to none, and to this the map of Israel is the highest witness. Yet the magnitude of the inheritance, both in its current physical dimensions and in its broader historical perspectives, is above all a challenge—a challenge no less inspiring, nor less exacting, than that which faced the founders.

The only real significance of the past is the extent to which it can strengthen those who, identifying themselves with its obligations as well as its inspiration, move with both of them into the future.

PART 2

HOW IT WORKS

It isn't the kibbutz which has to examine itself to see whether it is following the Marxist path, but rather the Marxists who have to check their own premises in light of the experience of the kibbutz way of life.

JEAN-PAUL SARTRE, March 1967

CHAPTER 1

The Interdependence of Functions in Kibbutz Society

In DEFINING the kibbutz, it is customary to use such expressions as a "new society" or a "new way of life". It is precisely this, and to call the kibbutz a communal farm, though it is no less true, is only part of the truth. To a student who has no special knowledge of the subject, it is probably easier to explain what a tree is, than to provide him with a general conception of the nature of a forest. For though a forest is made up of a large number of separate trees, it is more than their sum total, and a knowledge of trees is not necessarily synonymous with an understanding of forests and forestry.

HOW TO SEE BOTH THE TREES AND THE WOOD

To present the kibbutz in its entirety, it is necessary to see its detailed functioning as a new society with its own ideological, economic, social, educational, moral and spiritual principles. It is equally important to know the nature of these tenets and standards, to see how they work out in the practice of daily life, and to understand the relationship between them. This last aspect presents special difficulties: perhaps this is why visitors dropping into the kibbutz for a few hours and failing to perceive the different dimensions of kibbutz life come away with such different impressions.

A tourist who saw my kibbutz only on Saturday morning, when parents and children relaxed on shady lawns enjoying their day of rest together, summed it up as a human Paradise. His friend, who arrived on the morrow, in the middle of a summer working-day, when people toiled in the fields under Israel's broiling sun, thought that it must be Hell in the Kibbutz!

Had they both lived and worked in a kibbutz for any length of time, they would have gained more correct and unified impressions. But the problem is, of course, far deeper than this, and it can be well summarised by going back to the original metaphor and noting that in the kibbutz it is hard to see the wood for the trees. This is outstandingly true for the casual visitor; it is often true for outside specialists (economists, sociologists, psychologists, etc.) concentrating in their research on kibbutz life on one particular aspect and trying to fit it into their pre-formed notions. If some of these "experts"—both those who approach the kibbutz with a more or less open mind and those whose essential approach is hostile—frequently draw wrong conclusions, this is hardly surprising. For within the kibbutz itself and among those living in its reality, one of the main problems is that they, too, often find it hard to see the wood for the trees.

Both kibbutz life, and the kibbutz way of life, are extraordinarily dependent upon the unity of all the spheres of life and activity making up the sum total. This general truth is not, as some might claim, part of an ideological superstructure divorced from the daily life of kibbutz members. On the contrary, it does much to explain many of the most difficult and important of the daily social problems of kibbutz members and their community, and it also indicates how the working of kibbutz society, with all its economic, social and ideological ramifications, stands or falls according to the degree of unity, integration and interdependence between one sphere and another.

PARTS AND WHOLE

A successful kibbutz is not only a successful economic unit, social unit or educational-ideological unit. It must be all these and more. If its social unity and cohesion is undermined, this must inevitably have its effects on the economic and educational spheres of its activity. If its economic goals are not reached, this will be reflected in its social life and morale. If it cannot educate its children effectively in its own values, then clearly this will affect its whole future. (Lest we be misunderstood, we should add that the effect of an economic crisis, for example, could be either to strengthen or to weaken the social cohesion. It is the interdependence which is undeniable, and at this stage we are stating no more than this.)

As an illustration, let us take the following comparatively simple example of the relationship between work and economic factors on the one hand, and social values on the other. The income of the kibbutz is used to provide all the members with goods and services —housing, food, etc. There is no individual remuneration as we know it in systems of wage-labour. All the members benefit equally in the provision of their material needs from the fruits of the kibbutz economy.

What would happen if changes took place in the social life of the kibbutz which convinced a member that this principle of equality had been undermined to such an extent that though he was *giving equally* of his labour and energy, he was not *receiving equally* from the commune? His main conclusion might well be that in this situation there would be no purpose in his continuing to give of his best in order to advance the kibbutz economy. The result would be that in his place of work, the work would be done unsatisfactorily, and this would have its negative consequences in the economic life of the kibbutz.

It is true that this example is something of an over-simplification. Even so, it may serve to show the degree of interdependence which exists between two aspects of kibbutz life, the economic and the social. Further illustrations would show that this interdependence extends over kibbutz life in its entirety and without exception, encompassing the whole gamut of its complicated material and spiritual range of activities. The structure of the commune is such that only a very high degree of unity between the various spheres, and of identification between the kibbutz member and each one of them, can enable the system as a whole to function.

INTERDEPENDENCE AND IDENTIFICATION

It is not always easy to see the wood for the trees, because kibbutz members—though they are objectively involved in everything which goes on within the life of the kibbutz—are naturally more involved in one sphere than another, depending on their place of work, their inclinations, etc. In so far as there are clashes between members and groups of members, these are frequently an expression of what looks to them like schisms, or antagonisms, between different spheres.

It is natural that in the annual discussion preceding the drawing up of the kibbutz budget there will be different demands from members whose primary interests lie in a particular sphere, be it agriculture or industry, education or culture. Similarly, it would be unrealistic to expect that there will not be those who stress the need to raise the standard of living of the members and those who would give priority to investment in the productive sectors of the economy. Such a discussion is a function of the real and objective problems of kibbutz life. It is influenced, however, by subjective factors such as the particular branch in which a member works or the particular office which he is holding.

A high degree of ability to see both the particular tree and the whole wood is mandatory in order to maintain the delicate balance in kibbutz life between various spheres of activity, between them and the members responsible for them, and between the members themselves.

There are, as we shall see, various sources to this unity within kibbutz life and those for whom its problems are the stuff of their daily lives and not only the subject for research. The primary source can only be found in the voluntary *identification* of the member with the commune and with the tenets upon which it is founded, democratically determined by a full and frank exchange of views in which every effort is made to reach a *concensus of opinion*.

The purpose is to ensure that this concensus is as broad as possible and as representative as possible. This depends on maximum participation in the discussion and upon a readiness to respect different shades of opinion and to incorporate them into the ultimate decision. Such a democratic process is often long drawn-out, but this is a price demanded by the kibbutz system. Once resolved, the decision is binding on all, even though those who remain of a different opinion may continue to argue it internally.

This is what is called ideological collectivism (*collectiviut rayonit*) in the Kibbutz Artzi. Without it, the commune would disintegrate; its degree of internal cohesion is almost identical with this degree of identification; its strength or weakness in all spheres of activity, including the balance between them and their underlying unity, can neither be measured nor understood in terms of other criteria.

In order to see how the kibbutz system works, we shall look at the various aspects of its many-sided operation one by one. Yet, as we study the trees, it would be well to remember that the wood is, as we have said, far more than their sum total. Each tree is dependent upon and influenced by its neighbour. This is not only the core of some of the difficulties involved in explaining the kibbutz to those who have not lived its life; at the same time, it is close to the roots of many of the dilemmas of kibbutz society itself.

CHAPTER 2

The Socio-Economic Basis of Kibbutz

IN HIS pamphlet, *Communal Farming in Israel*, Yosef Shatil explains the socio-economic framework of the kibbutz as follows:

> Communal settlements are collective enterprises. Farming and all other economic activities of a kibbutz are managed as one unit with a joint account, so that there are no individual household accounts. The members eat in a common dining-hall and have all their major and minor needs (housing, furniture, clothes and laundry, culture and recreation, medical care and all forms of social welfare, as well as cigarettes, toilet requisites, etc.) provided from a central source. Apart from a small yearly allowance for use outside the kibbutz (holidays, presents and so on), they receive no cash, and no money is paid to them in the form of wages.
>
> Work in the communal services (such as the kitchen, laundry and clothes-store) is integrated into the general work organization of the settlement. Women are equal members in the organization, doing equal work and having an equal voice in kibbutz management. In most kibbutzim, including all those of the Kibbutz Artzi, children of all ages— from infancy through adolescence—live in their own houses, those of each age-group living together in their own units, which combine bedrooms, playrooms and classrooms. The children spend afternoons and the weekly Sabbath with their parents.
>
> The kibbutz is not a cooperative. There are no entrance fees, no individual shares in the common property and no individual accounts. If a new member is accepted, he is entitled to his full share in expenditure from the general budget, and has full voting rights. On the other hand, if a member leaves the settlement, he has no claim on the common property, though he will get some assistance to help him through the transition to life outside the kibbutz. All ownership is invested in the group as such, independent of its temporary personal composition.
>
> The basic ideas in the "constitution" of the kibbutz are purely voluntary membership and participation, along with equal and common respon-

sibility. Anyone may apply for membership, and the group is free to accept or to refuse his application. Any member may leave if he so decides, irrespective of his reasons. There are no punitive measures applied within the kibbutz apart from very infrequent cases of expulsion.

In an average settlement more than half the members share direct responsibility for operation of the kibbutz. There is therefore a very high degree of democracy within the group.*

COMPLETE COLLECTIVISM

The basic principles of the kibbutz are formulated as follows by H. Darin-Drabkin in his book, *Patterns of Co-operative Agriculture in Israel.*†

The kibbutz is a voluntary society based on both communal property, production and labour, and on communal consumption and living arrangements. In other words, the kibbutz community is responsible for the satisfaction of the individual's needs. "From each according to his ability, to each according to his needs", in accordance with the community's means—this is the principle underlying the unique socio-economic form that constitutes the Israeli kibbutz. Thus the kibbutz is fundamentally different from other cooperative enterprises in Israel or anywhere else in the world.

The unique character of the kibbutz is reflected, first and foremost, in its complete, even extreme, collectivist nature. No private property or private economic activity is allowed. Moreover, this all-embracing collectivism includes the cultural, social and educational spheres no less than the various economic aspects of kibbutz life. This all-embracing collectivist characteristic of kibbutz life is particularly conspicuous in four main spheres: in the organisation of work and production; in ownership of property; in consumption; and in the education of children.

---

* Taken, with minor changes, from *Communal Farming in Israel*, by Y. Shatil of Kibbutz Hazorea, reprinted by Hashomer Hatzair in New York from an article in the quarterly journal, *Land Economics* of May 1955. See also the same author's *L'Economie Collective du Kibboutz Israelienne*, Editions de Minuit, Paris, 1960.

† Published by the Department for International Co-operation, Ministry of Foreign Affairs, for the International Association for Rural Planning, Israel Institute for Books, Tel Aviv, 1962.

PRINCIPLES OF ECONOMIC ACTION

In order to explain the essentials of kibbutz economy, we must start by pointing out that the kibbutz differs from a capitalistic enterprise not only in its internal social organisation, but above all in its principles of economic action.* Shatil writes that

one may visualise it as a combination between a family enterprise which works for its own subsistence and a public enterprise which serves some civic purpose. In both cases, maximum profits are not the prime purpose, but rather the wish, in the first case, to attain and maintain a certain standard of living; and in the second case, to provide optimal service to the community at reasonable economic cost.

The Kibbutz aims to fulfil certain national purposes like colonisation, development of agricultural resources, increase of agricultural production, industrialisation, transition of people remote from physical labour to work on the land and the defence of the country. Together with this, it wishes to attain a decent standard of living for its members. All these tasks have priority over the striving for profit. A kibbutz will settle in a new and undeveloped area, rather than a populated area where economic prospects would be better. It will increase production and continue development as long as the average return pays minimum expense of living and interest on outside capital. New settlements are frequently situated in spots dictated by strategic needs rather than economic viability.

On the other hand, its need to attain economic independence limits the kibbutz. Unlike a public enterprise, it cannot make the consumer or the public purse pay for deficits. It is in direct competition with private enterprise. It receives some credits for development from Zionist institutions and from the State, but no subsidies other than those given to agriculture in general. The kibbutz must balance its annual budget and strive for self-subsistence. Only within these limits is it free to fulfil its national and social tasks. A new kibbutz knows from the first day of its settlement that it has to earn its own living.

These principles of economic action have two main consequences. First, the accumulation of capital is slow. There are, of course, good and bad times, and a good year brings profit to the kibbutz. Second, in the use of outside capital the kibbutz does not calculate, like a capitalist

* See Y. Shatil's pamphlet *Communal Farming in Israel*, and also *The Economic Basis of the Kibbutz*, by Eliezer Hacohen of Kibbutz Beith Alfa, published by the Afro-Asian Institute for Labour Studies and Co-operation, from both of which we have quoted freely in these pages.

enterprise, whether borrowed capital will in every case leave a profit after interest has been paid. Sometimes, it is sufficient if a loan serves to develop the farm, or industry, and facilitates the employment of additional workers from among the members, including older people no longer able to work in heavy agricultural jobs. For a kibbutz, profit-maximisation is not its first and chief aim, but rather the development of the community and of the country as a whole.

To sum up, therefore, the difference between a kibbutz and a capitalist enterprise within the same money economy lies in the quite different social purposes of the two units. Capital aims at profit for its own sake, for the purpose of capital accumulation. The kibbutz aims at economic viability in order to fulfil its national and social purposes and provide for the needs of its members, material and non-material. In order to pay for the necessary goods and services which it obtains on the general market, the kibbutz has to earn an income by selling its products on services at a price enabling it to cover its costs to provide a decent standard of living for the members and to leave a certain surplus wherever possible.

The purpose of the surplus is firstly to repay over the years the debts incurred in the establishment of the settlement and, secondly, to permit steady development, progress and expansion including that standard of living entailed in the kibbutz way of life—complete social security, full and equal educational opportunities for the young, etc. Many border kibbutzim have to reckon on paying high security expenses. This comparatively high standard of living (see p. 82) demands an efficient and expanding economic base.

MIXED FARM

The agricultural economy of the kibbutz is founded on *intensive mixed farming on a large scale*, avoiding the agricultural and economic disadvantages of big one-crop farming as well as the low productivity of the small family farm. Nowadays a "kibbutz-family", like all settlers, gets about 7–8 acres of irrigated land or its equivalent in land for dry-farming.

A communal farm in Israel usually has between 100 and 200 of these family units—the most frequent number is 120—combined together. A family farm with one cow, up to a hundred chickens, half an acre of vegetable garden and half an acre of fruit trees might have a low level of production and will make rather a meagre living. Multiplied by a hundred, this is sufficient for modern and rational farming methods, with each branch large enough to allow for a considerable measure of mechanisation.

Large-scale organisation facilitates high productivity through a rational division of labour, specialisation and the use of scientific methods, modern machinery and improved techniques. The devotion of the private farmer to his small plot and his livestock, motivated by his own self-interest, needs no explanation: but the potential advantages of large-scale production must be allied to an equivalent motivation on the part of the kibbutz member. Without this, the built-in advantages of the larger unit can be dissipated. The kibbutz way of life seems to provide this motivation.

Mixed farming is essential for the development of agricultural production within a sound national economy. Monoculture, single-crop agriculture, plantations providing cheap raw materials and foodstuffs produced exclusively for exports to "developed" countries—these are the signs of a colonial economy. Exclusive specialisation in export crops—according to the principle of comparative advantage, can lead to a distortion of the correct basis of healthy agriculture, which must look after home needs first. The diversification of agriculture is well illustrated by the kibbutz farm which does not exclude specialisation so as to make the best use of local advantages but sets out to exploit the proven benefits of mixed farming: the distribution of risk—financial losses through natural causes like drought or pests, or market fluctuations; and branches complementing each other as regards crop-rotation.

Crops are planned so as to make the best possible use of land and water resources. A high degree of self-sufficiency in food supply has vital security implications for a small country like Israel surrounded by hostile states. Finally, the mixed farm makes possible more equal distribution of labour during the whole year—a factor of special importance to the kibbutz as it must provide work for all its members at all times.

A diversified agricultural and industrial economy gives larger scope for the abilities and inclinations of those who make up the community. The right man must be in the right job but a man must have the job to which he as an individual is interested. Though the kibbutz work structure has its limitations—especially for the woman—the more varied its economy the greater are the chances of satisfying the needs of members in their work. In a society whose motivations are so different from those accepted elsewhere, because wage inducements are completely unknown, this is a matter of special importance.

There are several main branches of agriculture in the kibbutzim, including grain farming, green fodder, deciduous fruits and bananas, citrus, industrial crops such as cotton and sugar-beet, and livestock: cows, chickens and sheep. Their relative importance depends upon regional conditions, which also determine the addition of other branches like fishing (on the coasts, in lakes and primarily in artificial ponds), flowers, bees, melons, etc.

As we have noted, Israel is a tiny country with limited natural resources, striving for maximum employment on a minimum plot of land. The kibbutz is especially adapted to this purpose because it can exploit every modern and scientific method; efficient irrigation, the introduction of new crops and experimentation, improvement of seeds, use of fertilisers, better crop rotation, product refinement, high yields and high returns. However, there are limits to agricultural intensification and the law of diminishing returns dictates that at a certain point, additional use of capital no longer yields an adequate return. While many categories of outside work are undertaken by kibbutz members, the main outlet is to be found in industrial development.

INDUSTRY

With the expansion of population in the settlements and as they sought for additional sources of work and income, industry has grown rapidly, so that overall income from kibbutz industry amounts to about a third of the total, and over half in some kibbutzim. About 7000 people work in kibbutz industrial plants—2·6 per cent of Israel's industrial manpower—and this figure is growing year by year. They produce about 5·3 per cent of the country's industrial output, and a quarter of that in the Histradrut sector. These figures (for 1966) include regional industries, such as cotton-gins, owned by all the kibbutzim in the area.

Their products extend over the widest range, including agricultural machinery and irrigation pipes, furniture and plastic goods, electrical equipment and precision instruments, paints and ceramics, clothing, foodstuffs and bicycles, to give only a few examples. There are more than 150 small and medium factories in the kibbutzim, apart from workshops, garages and carpentry shops which often take on outside work.

Hundreds of the settlements' trucks are organised in transport co-operatives for general haulage; kibbutz bulldozers and heavy tractors work all over the country; and there are many other categories of outside work done by men and machines. These non-agricultural branches strengthen the economic base of the settlements, provide a living for more people on the same limited land resources and do away with complete dependence on agriculture, with all its seasonal hazards.

The division of that half of the labour force in the Kibbutz Artzi settlements working in income-producing branches (excluding those services not connected with productive branches) was as follows:

	Labour force	Percentage in agriculture	Percentage in industry	Percentage in outside work
1962	8530	69·7	15·2	15·1
1964	8850	67·2	16·4	16·4
1966	9190	64·5	17·4	18·1

Outside work refers to places of work not owned by an individual kibbutz—regional industry, government and Histadrut institutions, etc.

THE SERVICES

About half of the members of a kibbutz are occupied in the services—kitchen, laundry, clothes-store, nursing, education, etc. However, this more or less equal division between production and services does not give the whole picture, for kibbutz services provide not only for the usual needs of a family household, but also for many additional items which the latter would normally buy.

Clothes and shoes are not only repaired but often made in the kibbutz. Carpenter, mechanic, plumber, electrician and others— all are kibbutz members working both in maintenance and in new investments. Those in education include house-mothers, the teaching-staff of the kibbutz kindergarten, primary and secondary schools—altogether 36 per cent of the female working-force in the K.A.

A kibbutz may improve its living standards without additional cash expenditure simply by the transfer of workers to service branches. Yet it is clear that the relationship between productive and non-productive work has a decisive influence on the economic viability of the kibbutz, and an exaggerated concentration of workers in the services can only be at the expense of the production branches on which direct profitability is founded. Were the ratio of "income-earning" to "non-income earning" working-days to fall below a certain level, the advantages of the kibbutz system and its chances of profitability would be frittered away. To find the correct balance is one of the important functions of those responsible for planning the kibbutz economy.

WORK AND MANPOWER

In its rational use of available manpower, the kibbutz structure facilitates a high degree of organisation and planning even if this is not always exploited to the maximum. All work is carried out according to an overall plan, incorporating all categories of available "working-days", submitted annually by the work committee to the members' meeting and broken down into smaller monthly, weekly and daily plans. The usual working day for men is 8–9 hours. Mothers of two children and all women over the age of 35 work a 7-hour day. Older people work a shorter day according to a sliding scale until retirement.

The work plan takes into account every type of work, in production and services alike and every category of worker: male and female members; older people, youth groups and children who work a few hours a day according to their age; work camps from Israel and abroad; temporary groups training or learning in the kibbutz; soldiers of Nachal★ units and Ulpan★ students; visitors spending some weeks or months in the kibbutz, etc.

The daily work rota or schedule (*Sidur Avoda* in Hebrew), worked out during the day and placed on the notice-board in the evening for the following day, is the nerve centre of the kibbutz. The work organiser, whose task is rotated between members elected for some months or a year, must translate the overall plan into all its numerous details, balancing the needs of the various branches and services so as to try and satisfy all their many needs and demands.

This is a task requiring organisational ability and human understanding (along with strong nerves!), for the maximum possible satisfaction of members in their work is a basic social principle of the voluntary-democratic kibbutz society. It is also vital for the efficient functioning of the economy. Since some of the work in agriculture and the services is particularly boring and unpopular, every effort is made to rotate the members working—and often grumbling—in these jobs.

The aim is to provide as many members as possible with permanent and satisfying work demanding skilled knowledge, and, indeed, less than 20 per cent of the labour force is at any time working in so-called "temporary places of work". Most of the members are therefore able to reach varying levels of skill in their work, and the kibbutz encourages them to advance through a wide variety of study and training-courses. The highly developed

★ Nachal—a unit of the Israel Army combining agricultural work and defence functions. Ulpan—Hebrew course for new immigrants whose day is equally divided between study and work.

kibbutz economy would, indeed, be impossible without constant concern to increase the expert knowledge of its workers everywhere.

Increasing attention has recently been given to the organisation and technical proficiency of individual branches, and to the democratic human relations between those working as a team within them. This, too, is equally dictated by economic and social needs, since only skilled workers happy in their jobs and fully conscious of the potential for improvement existing in all branches can secure their harmonious functioning and economic efficiency. In this respect, much remains to be done in some of the services and in so far as it is possible to generalise, men in the kibbutz are often happier in their work than women. Planning, seasonal flexibility and the devotion with which nearly all kibbutz members approach their work enable us to sum up that in its use of manpower the kibbutz enjoys definite advantages over other forms of settlement in Israel.

However, the high degree of organisation through which this is achieved in settlements almost chronically short of manpower creates tensions which cause many serious personal problems—such as incompatibility, frustration and dissatisfaction with the work assignment—and can have grave repercussions in the relationship of the individual to the commune. Every effort is made by individual kibbutzim and by the kibbutz movements to minimise these tensions, but they are not easily overcome in certain fields of work, including some where women are mainly occupied. On the efforts to find solutions to these questions depends to no small extent the ability of the kibbutz to satisfy the needs and aspirations of its members, young and old.

The wonderful traditions of work in the kibbutz movement, founded above all on the dignity of labour and the principle of equality, have done much to do away with the distinction so prevalent in other societies between various types of work.

Perhaps this was what Jean-Paul Sartre meant when he commented that

on kibbutz I found the realisation of the vision which Marx once expressed —that the day would come when the difference between the man who labours with his hands and the intellectuals would disappear. We saw in the kibbutz farmers who are at one and the same time intellectuals and workers. They are shepherds and are informed in literature, sociology and politics. This isn't so simple and there exists a dialectical contradiction in this area, but we found here a uniqueness in unity. [1957.]

This provides a sound basis for the hope that within the democratic kibbutz society, planning and organisation will go hand in hand with that understanding of human problems and that striving for human happiness achieved through releasing the creative potential of the individual, without which Socialism has no positive meaning for mankind.

ECONOMIC GUIDANCE

In the establishment and consolidation of its economy, as in all other major questions which determine its character and approach to the many dilemmas of kibbutz life, each settlement must tackle things in its own way, but it sets about this with the invaluable help and guidance of norms and precedents set by the appropriate department of the Kibbutz Artzi. The economic departments of the kibbutz movement are uniquely equipped to advise and direct the kibbutzim, as a result of many years' study and experience of every stage and facet in the economic development of the settlements. Thus the experience of others is brought home to each of the kibbutzim and they are spared errors of judgement which would be inevitable if every settlement were on its own. Kibbutz farmers also enjoy the expert advice of Ministry of Agriculture and Jewish Agency specialists.

This centralisation of advice and experience, equally important in all aspects of kibbutz life, and co-ordinated through the departments and central institutions of the movement, is now an integral part of the kibbutz system, and of prime importance and significance to all the settlements, and particularly to those facing the initial problems of development and consolidation of their economy.

THE HISTADRUT AND THE JEWISH NATIONAL FUND

Moreover, the kibbutzim constitute an important part of a wide network of co-operative institutions within the economy of Israel. The General Federation of Labour (*Histadrut*) is much more than a trade union organising about 80 per cent of the country's workers. By 1966 its membership reached the million mark and it served one and a half million people, 63 per cent of Israel's population. Over 60 per cent of the members are post-State immigrants. The *Histadrut* also has its own affiliated economic enterprises which include the kibbutzim, the *moshavim* (smallholders' co-operative settlements with a population of about 125,000), urban industrial co-operatives, *Solel Boneh* (Israel's largest contractor for building and public works), banks, etc. This sector accounts for about a quarter of the national economy and for 70 per cent of agriculture. It must be remembered that though Israel is a capitalist country, its public sector—the part owned by the Government, the Zionist institutions and the *Histadrut*—accounts for nearly half the G.N.P.

Thus the agricultural produce of the kibbutzim, as well as the moshavim, is marketed by *T'nuva*, which is a *Histradrut*-affiliated producers' co-operative marketing two-thirds of all Israel's farm produce. A parallel purchasing co-operative called *Hamashbir Hamerkazi* supplies them with means of production and consumer goods. Even though many of the economic activities of the *Histadrut* are the subject of strong controversy within the labour movement, the kibbutzim know that these marketing organisations serve them far better than they could expect if they were forced to sell their produce to the individual trader. If proof is needed it is to be found in the retail margin and the lack of benefit for the consumer when the producer's price goes down.

Whenever the kibbutz is dependent upon capitalist enterprise it knows that in the nature of class society this must be to the detriment of the commune, whereas the strengthening of the public—and particularly the workers' sector of the economy—is to its advantage.

Additional evidence of this is to be found in the vital area of *land ownership*. Some 90 per cent of land in Israel is nationalised, and agricultural land is the property of the nation through a joint body of the Government and the Jewish National Fund. It is leased to the settlers for forty-nine years, after which time the contract is prolonged on condition that the land is exploited according to the contract, which makes self-labour by the farmer a condition of the lease. The farmers pay a relatively low rent on the lease.

In contrast, land speculation is rife in urban areas, where private individuals and companies exploit their ownership in order that maximum profits accrue, regardless of the national interest. In this way, tracts of land suitable for agriculture have been used without any justification for other purposes, and capitalist landowners have made phenomenal profits from real estate.

Fortunately, the landownership problem of the kibbutzim and of other forms of agriculture found its solution outside the framework of capitalist speculation and profiteering through the vital work of the Jewish National Fund.

CHAPTER 3

The Kibbutz Economy in Action

THERE is a wealth of statistical material providing evidence that the kibbutz as an economic unit enjoys advantages in productivity within Israeli agriculture. Since the creation of the State, the kibbutz economy has gone through various phases, as has the economy of Israel in general. The sellers' market of the early 1950's, when farmers had to strain themselves to feed the quickly growing population, gave way to the appearance at the end of the 1950's of agricultural surpluses which challenged the profitability of Israel's expanding agriculture.

After weathering this crises, kibbutz agriculture of the 1960's, carefully planned to meet home needs and with stress on industrial crops, products for canning and above all expansion of exports, appears to be one of the most efficient and productive sectors of the Israeli economy. Three-quarters of Israel's food is now produced at home.

It should be borne in mind that comparisons between the kibbutz and the moshav, which together dominate Israel's agriculture, can be misleading. Both are a part of the Histadrut sector (the labour economy) which produces 70 per cent of the country's agricultural output. In 1965 the moshav, with a total population of 124,330, produced 55 per cent of this, the kibbutz (population 80,558) 45 per cent. But though both are *Histadrut*-affiliated and share the very general concept of a Labour Israel, *the socio-economic purposes of the two forms of settlement are very different.*

The way of life of the moshav farmer is quite different from that in the kibbutz. Though the moshav practices mutual aid between members, there is no mutual responsibility as in the collective. The moshav member finds it hard to take that vacation guaranteed in the kibbutz; the moshav woman works without fixed hours and the man is often busy from sunrise to sunset. Neither can he enjoy the training facilities available to the kibbutz farmer. In the moshav, all is orientated towards making the farm profitable while in the kibbutz, though this is a high priority, not everything is subordinated to it. Statistical comparisons between settlements of the two types must therefore be understood in their context of different aims as well as different internal organisation. Because of the small unit in the moshav farm, it is facing a structural crisis, while the problems of the kibbutz are quite different.

In his valuable book *The Other Society* (Victor Gollancz, 1962), Dr. H. Darin-Drabkin pointed out that between 1949 and 1959, while the number of workers in the kibbutzim increased by 31 per cent their agricultural production rose 3·6 times. Comparison with other countries shows that whereas forty to eighty years are normally required to raise agricultural output 2–3 times, the kibbutz succeeded in raising output per worker roughly 4 times in twenty years.

More recent figures are quoted in *The Economy of the Israeli Kibbutz* by Eliyahu Kanovsky (Harvard Middle East Monograph Series, Harvard University Press, 1966). He notes that

> as a result of their heavy investment in agriculture and their increasing proficiency, the collectives have generally succeeded in keeping pace with, and exceeding, the very high growth rates of Israeli agriculture. In 1964 Israel's agricultural production had increased to a level of 6 times its 1949 level (in real terms) and kibbutz agriculture was 7 times its 1949 level of production. The kibbutz share of total agricultural production in Israel has fluctuated between a low of 27·6 per cent in 1949 and a high of over 31 per cent reached in a number of years in the 1950's and between 1960 and 1964. . . . Between 1949–1960, productivity in kibbutz agriculture increased at an annual rate of 10 per cent. There is every sign that this rate of growth in productivity has been maintained or exceeded, on the average, between 1949 and 1964.

The author* goes on to note that the gap, formerly very large

* We are indebted to Kanovsky's work for some of the statistical material in this chapter. Our statistics are taken from the authorised institutions and publications of the Government, Central Bureau of Statistics, the *Histadrut*, and the Kibbutz Movement.

between the production per worker in the kibbutz and other sectors, has been narrowed by the recent improvements in the Moshav's efficiency.* He quotes a 1960 study showing that during the years 1953–8, kibbutz labour productivity (gross agricultural output per kibbutz agricultural worker) increased at an average rate of 12·2 per cent annually as against 7·3 per cent in Israel's agriculture as a whole.

In the Kibbutz Artzi settlements, 5,930 agricultural workers produced agricultural supplies to the value of I£105 million in 1961. With the same labour force, this went up in five years (1966) to I£155·4 million—over 50 per cent. In 1966 the Kibbutz Artzi settlements were producing 10·5 per cent of Israel's agricultural output (see Table 1).

TABLE 1

Year	Value of agric. output (I£)	Value of agric. output in K.A. (millions I£)	Rise in agric. productivity per worker in K.A.	Kibbutz Artzi per cent of total agric. output in Israel
1962	1027 milliard	105·6	8·3	10·3
1963	1218 milliard	118·6	7·4	9·7
1964	1320 milliard	134·4	10·7	10·2
1965	1424 milliard	146·7	8·1	10·3
1966	1481 milliard	155·4	0·4	10·5

THE KIBBUTZ CONTRIBUTION

In 1966 the kibbutzim were cultivating 31·7 per cent of land used for agriculture in Israel and 39·8 per cent of Jewish-owned land, including 33·7 per cent of all irrigated land. Looking at individual agricultural branches, in 1966 the kibbutzim were

* The agricultural worker in the Moshav produced about 53 per cent of that of his kibbutz counterpart in 1957, 71 per cent in 1960. Total output grew in 1959–61 by 41·9 per cent in the kibbutzim, 110·4 per cent in the moshavim. See also H. Nachshon's article in the *Economic Quarterly*, March 1963.

producing the percentages shown in Table 2 of Israel's Jewish agricultural output:

TABLE 2

	per cent		per cent
Wheat	62	Citrus	12
Barley	25	Bananas	89
Sorghum (corn)	64	All fruit	74
Hay	78	Milk	41
Cotton	70	Beef	43
Sugar beet	37	Meat (poultry)	34
Vegetables	7	Eggs	13
Potatoes	38	Honey	25
Fish (from fish ponds)	91		

In dairying, 1963 yields per cow in the kibbutzim were 22 per cent higher than for the rest of Israel's herds. Litres of milk per workday have risen in the kibbutzim between 1949 and 1960 from 129 to 503, an annual growth of 13·2 per cent. Another study showed that in 1960 yields per cow in the kibbutz were 75 per cent above those in the dairy branch in England, with double the output per labourday in the kibbutz. Kibbutz dairy herds give yields among the highest in the world; they are able to exploit mechanisation and scientific feeding methods and benefit from large units and modern installations.

Similar advantages are enjoyed by the poultry branch in the kibbutzim. In 1959, with 16 per cent of the laying hens they were producing 21·7 per cent of eggs. The number of eggs per laying hen was some 25 per cent higher in the kibbutz sector. In the large modern coops usual in the kibbutzim one worker can take care of about 3 times the number of chickens in the small or medium coops prevalent in the moshav.

Turning to field crops and industrial crops—the latter is an important recent addition to kibbutz farming—the figures in Table 3 show the number of labour-hours required to produce a metric ton of produce in the kibbutzim.

TABLE 3

Year	Wheat	Green fodder (irrigated)	Hay	Potatoes	Cotton	Sugar beet
1949	36·8	11·2	17·6	74·4		
1958	24	6·4	13·6	46·4	138·4 (1960)	16
1966	10–12	2–4	10–11	10–11	30–35	5–6

In all agricultural operations where large-scale farming and mechanisation can be used, the kibbutz enjoys advantages; conversely in those crops, like vegetables, which need much manual labour the family farm is at an advantage. The composition of agricultural output in the Kibbutz Artzi (in the other kibbutz movements there are only slight variations) in 1964 are shown in Table 4.

TABLE 4

Poultry	21 per cent
Fruit (including citrus)	22·9 per cent
Dairying	19·1 per cent
Field crops (grains)	13·8 per cent
Industrial crops and fodder	13·2 per cent
Fishing	7·5 per cent
Vegetables and potatoes	2·5 per cent

The collectives pioneered the modernisation and intensification of Israeli agriculture. Lately, however, the higher rate of mechanisation in the non-kibbutz sector has reduced the formerly very high relative share of agricultural machinery owned by the kibbutzim but they have more of the sophisticated agricultural machinery.

In 1966 the kibbutz movement was producing 30 per cent of Israel's agricultural output. In agricultural productivity and mechanisation, the kibbutzim have reached a level more or less on a par with the advanced Western Europeanc ountries but much lower than that of the U.S.A.

One expert has expressed the view that in order to gauge the importance of the kibbutz contribution to the national economy, it can be reckoned that agriculture—the most basic part of the occupational structure of the people—provides work in industry and auxiliary services for another two to three breadwinners. If we assume that some 50 per cent of the breadwinners (this excludes administration) are engaged in work connected in one way or another with the agricultural base, some 15 per cent are dependent on kibbutz agriculture. To this one must add kibbutz industry, with its auxiliary occupations. Accordingly, if about 4 per cent of the population lives in the kibbutz, it creates an occupational base for about five times more people—about a fifth of the total working population. The author, Knesset member Zeev Tsur of the Kibbutz Hameuchad's Sdeh Nahum, adds that the kibbutzim also play a role out of proportion to their size in the army, in securing the borders, in the labour movement, in the education of Jewish youth in Israel and abroad, in the political life of the country, etc. (See *Mibifnim*, in Hebrew, November 1963.)

It must not be forgotten that while private farming in Israel usually concentrates in the central regions of the country and near the towns, and in those agricultural branches promising the quickest returns and highest profits, the location and agricultural structure of the kibbutzim were motivated by national needs. Thus they concentrated on mixed farming in order to feed the growing population, and went out to remote and undeveloped areas. Guarding the borders and pioneering the development of these regions for further settlement, they built up their economy in unfavourable economic circumstances.

Future colonisation in Israel must be directed primarily towards certain hilly regions which may provide some settlement possibilities in the North, but above all to the deep South, which private capital will avoid and where even the moshav might face grave initial difficulties. Here again, the communal type of settlement can provide a key to the expansion of agricultural and industrial development in the vast tracts—a half of Israel's territory—still awaiting redemption. Again, we are referring to Israeli territory as of the 1949 borders without touching upon areas occupied by Israel during the Six-Day War of 1967.

CHARACTERISTICS OF KIBBUTZ INDUSTRY

The Israel economy is rapidly becoming more industrialised, while at the same time technological progress enables less people to produce more food on the same land, and in the kibbutz, as in all Israel's agriculture, the amount of land and water available is strictly limited. Elsewhere, both abroad and in the Israeli moshav, high productivity and government-imposed production quotas often result in the necessity for many of the grown-up sons of the farming population to move from the country to the town. The kibbutz's answer is the development of industry alongside its agricultural branches. It has the possibility of basing its economy upon *a combination of agricultural and industrial development*. This, the *flexibility* of the kibbutz economy, is one of its most important positive characteristics.

It is this which enables the kibbutz to absorb new members (and especially its own second generation) productively through *industrialisation without urbanisation*. The conditions of Israel make industrialisation imperative, but if this entails an exaggerated concentration in urban centres it presents a constant threat to the country's security and to the social stability of the population in outlying districts, near the borders and in development areas.

Because Israel has limited natural resources for industrial development in a competitive world, much depends on the skill and initiative of its industry. Experience has shown that the kibbutz worker brings to his work in the factory the same sense of identification and devotion as in agriculture. Y. Levitzky, a government productivity expert, has noted the team spirit, mutual confidence and readiness to make decisions which characterise kibbutz industry.

He writes that "kibbutz members who go into industry as skilled workers reveal interest and initiative which stand out in the introduction of improvements and efficient working-methods. It is a fact that in general not only does productivity in kibbutz industry not fall below that of the private sector, but on the contrary it is much higher."

The Minister of Commerce and Industry in the Israeli Government, Mr. Tsadok, noted in 1965 that

> to succeed in the great task of industrial development we must mobilise the ability of the kibbutz in enterprise, administration and organisation. The kibbutz movement has a great accumulation of ability in these areas. Its social structure provides fertile ground for the growth of teams of people who show the promise and practical ability to build healthy and efficient industry. . . . Kibbutz industrial products are of high quality and successfully compete at home and abroad. This is because of the good name they have won for themselves, especially in wood and plywood, ceramics, rubber, plastics, canned vegetables, irrigation equipment and agricultural machinery.

It is noteworthy that as regards industrial exports, on which so much of Israel's economic future depends, kibbutz industry is ahead of other sectors. Twenty per cent of its output went to direct and indirect exports in 1965 as against 16 per cent for the whole of industry (and only 10 per cent without diamonds).

It goes without saying that the introduction of industry into the kibbutzim on such a large and growing scale—by 1966, 82 per cent of the K.A. population lived in kibbutzim with industries and younger settlements are moving towards industrialisation as soon as their demographic situation permits—raises a whole series of problems which will have a large say in shaping the social, as well as the economic, image of the kibbutz in the future. In the kibbutz, the classical incentives of capitalist industry are wholly irrelevant. So are some aspects of industrial relations in state-owned plants, including Socialist countries (piece-work).

Looking at kibbutz industry as an integral part of the commune, it is clear that within this type of factory, "management" and "labour" as separate and watertight, not to speak of hostile entities, are wholly incompatible. The social implications of this are manifest: the need for democratic decisions at all levels, for rotation in management, for genuine and equal opportunities to advance through study, etc. This, no less than the economic test, will determine the future trends and success of kibbutz industry.

The kibbutz has not restricted itself to industry directly connected with agriculture. Table 5 is a breakdown of Israeli and kibbutz industry in 1965 according to branches.

TABLE 5

	Israeli industry percentage	Kibbutz industry percentage
Rubber, plastics, chemicals	9·5	14·5
Metal, electrical and transportation equipment	15·8	25·4
Basic metals and pipes	2·4	—
Wood, carpentry	8·2	29·2
Food	18·4	18·2
Textiles, clothing, leather	20·3	2·3
Domestic equipment	9·3	3·0
Diamonds	5·9	—
Refineries	3·3	—
Mining	2·3	—

The rate and direction of expansion in kibbutz industry in the 1960's is illustrated for the years 1963–5 in Table 6. The output value is in millions of Israeli pounds.

In general, kibbutz industry has been expanding during the 1960's by 15–30 per cent annually, compared to agriculture's 10 per cent. The recession had its negative effect on kibbutz industry: the figures for growth of output in kibbutz industry were 35 per cent in 1962, 31 in 1963, 14·8 in 1964, 17·0 in 1965 and 14·4 in 1966, a recession year. One observer has noted that if this growth continues, income from agriculture, now two-thirds, and from industry, now about a third, may be equal within a decade. In the veteran K.A. settlements, industry represents 40 per cent of production, over 50 per cent of the surplus.

Israel's industry is, in international standards, small-scale and factories employing many hundreds of workers are the exception.

Nevertheless, some critics believe that the kibbutz is at a disadvantage in competition with private or publicly owned factories

TABLE 6

Branch	Number of enterprises			Total output		
	1963	1964	1965 (July)	1963	1964	1965
Metal and machines	51	52	55	45	46	52
Wood	15	15	17	50	60	68
Food and chemicals	18	20	23	50	53	55
Plastics, leather, textiles	22	24	26	25	37	48
Building materials	12	13	13	10	11	13
Printing	4	4	4	3	3	3
Bakeries	4	4	4	3	3	3
Miscellaneous	4	4	4	4	4	5
TOTAL	131	136	145	190	217	247
Rest-homes	30	20	20	10	11	13
SUM TOTAL	151	156	165	200	228	260

because of its lack of manoeuvrability in manpower. A kibbutz cannot "lay off" large numbers of workers if this is called for in bad times and there are clear limits to its expansion potential in good times. The problem of hired labour is particularly acute in some kibbutz industries (see p. 188).

In order to ensure that the principle of self-labour shall apply to industry as well as agriculture, the K.A. has discouraged over-large factories, primarily dependent on hired workers. Most of its industry is in the small or medium category in Israeli standards— up to 40 workers (there are nine factories in the kibbutzim with over 100 workers). Figures do not bear out the theory that this policy impedes the development of viable and profitable industry. The contrary seems to be true: kibbutz industry is more efficient in general than its urban counterpart, and the K.A. does not seem to be the least efficient or profitable sector within kibbutz industry.

In 1964 the K.A., 34·2 per cent of the kibbutz movement, produced 34·7 per cent of agricultural output and 37·1 of industrial output.

The output per worker was I £26,000 in Israeli industry
The output per worker was I £31,800 in kibbutz industry as a whole
The output per worker was I £39,000 in Kibbutz Artzi industry

It may well be that precisely because a factory is planned from the start within a definite manpower limitation in mind—rather than on flexible numbers of unskilled workers—it is more likely to achieve those higher levels of mechanisation and know-how which augment its competitivity. Joint ownership by neighbouring kibbutzim, as is practised in the well-known Hazorea furniture plant, may be seen as a way to solve manpower problems without hired labour.

To sum up, we can see that kibbutz industry is not without its limitations and it cannot play the sort of quantative role in industry as it enjoys in agriculture. Yet the evidence indicates that it can more than hold its own against its private competitors. Its structure has some inherent advantages: long experience in agricultural production, a well-educated population with a strong technical bent in the younger generation, a high degree of work-morality and identification with the job, the possibility of introducing a constant process of learning for workers in industry of all ages and the development of an atmosphere of team spirit and co-operative responsibility in the factory.

In these directions, some observers see a new pioneering role for the kibbutz in an Israeli economy and society in which industrialisation and automation are signs of the times. In their opinion, the kibbutz can provide an example of modern, planned and democratically managed industry and this can influence other sectors as well.

The rapid growth of kibbutz industry will undoubtedly continue in the years to come, not at the expense of agriculture but side by side with it. The vision of large and growing communal villages founded on a combination of agriculture and industry is well on the way to realisation.

Conclusion
EFFICIENCY AND PROFITABILITY

We have tried in the preceding pages to show the advantages of the kibbutz form of economic organization in stimulating productivity in agriculture and industry. This is possible in the kibbutz system because of the unusual degree of planning, mechanisation and rationalisation in its large-scale mixed-farming operations; because of its success in promoting cadres capable of applying the latest agro-technical developments to the problems of Israel's agriculture; and to the kibbutz's ability to diversify through industrialisation, in which the same principles of economic action so effective in agriculture are again proving themselves.

The kibbutz system stands or falls with the people putting it into practice. The individual in the kibbutz is generally interested in studying so as to learn to do his work better, on a higher level. Though automation is not yet round the corner in Israel, it is on the way. The successful system will be that in which the individual is not afraid of automation, not threatened by it. The improvement of the work process in the collective cannot undermine the total security of the member—on the contrary, it raises both his status and his material gains if things are more efficient and profitable. This may help the kibbutz economy. As it moves forward, it will continue to depend on a unique combination of individual initiative, collective responsibility and growing know-how in an age of technological revolution. It is these which can explain past progress and hold out the promise of future achievements.

Technical productivity and profitability are not synonymous. In the kibbutz, the former is easily defined and measured whereas the latter is a cause of controversy among economists. One of the most authoritative kibbutz economists, Y. Shatil of Hazorea, points out that the surplus above living expenditures cannot be identified with savings in measuring kibbutz profitability. When the owner is also the operator, this type of calculation, sound as it may be in enterprises with external labour costs, is of no use. The decision on how to divide income between consumption and savings is only partially economic in the collective.

Economic efficiency does not always express itself in higher money-income. Labour can be expended on education, cultural activity or leisure and the kibbutz provides large opportunity for these types of "direct satisfactions". We have already noted that profit maximalisation is not the sole criterion of the kibbutz economy and neither did the kibbutz always adopt the early capitalistic virtue of "saving before consumption". Criticising E. Kanovsky's writings on kibbutz profitability,* Shatil challenges his criteria and objects to generalising from the particular position of the 1950's— which have already given way to a new and very different situation in the 1960's and will no doubt face different problems again in the 1970's.

It is a fact that the overall austerity which characterised kibbutz life in pre-State days is a thing of the past. Living standards rose in the 1950's parallel with the general trend in the country. In 1955 real living expenditures in the kibbutzim were about equal in retail prices, to those of the average wage-earner in Israel. The only study comparing real net income in a kibbutz and a moshav, made by Y. Lowe in the mid-1950's, concludes that taking into account the great internal differentiation within a moshav, and other differences, net income per family in the two types of settlement was about equal, with a much smaller labour-input per family in the kibbutz. The young kibbutz will earn more than the young moshav and the above is mainly true of established settlements.

Between 1961 and 1966 an average annual increase in consumption expenses of 5 per cent above the country's cost-of-living index has been recorded in the kibbutzim. In general, it is noteworthy that there are considerable differences between settlements in this respect and the age of a kibbutz is not always decisive for its profitability.

We have mentioned that from the middle 1950's, when the food shortage was overcome by an unparalleled expansive effort of Israel's farmers, agricultural surpluses have become a permanent feature of the situation. Since then, with Israel's population growing 3–4 per cent annually and agricultural production increasing by

* See the magazine *New Outlook*, September 1966.

10 per cent, the farmers faced a decline in profitability which reached its peak in 1959.

The 1960's present a picture fundamentally different from the decade before. Agriculture is nationally planned with each branch working according to production quotas for the whole country, divided up between the settlements. In addition to these administrative limitations, subsidies to agriculture grew (to a large extent in order to hold down the cost-of-living index). The kibbutz reaction to the new conditions was not only to expand its industrial branches but also to streamline its agricultural operations, concentrating on those branches which held out the best prospects in each settlement yet without giving up the principle of mixed farming. Though mistakes were certainly made, the overall direction seems to have been proven correct.

Of particular importance to the new look of the kibbutz economy has been the improvement of management and accounting techniques. Modern methods of planning and calculation of profitability are now commonplace. Many kibbutzim use the methods of linear planning to find optimum solutions for their distribution of productive resources. Furthermore, some rethinking of basic economic concepts was inevitable in order to grapple with the prospect of a limited home market, the emphasis on exports and the need for a far more careful investment policy.

Economic efficiency rather than sheer physical productivity now takes first place. The kibbutz economic manager, who has overall responsibility for directing the economy, now receives a far deeper training than used to be customary. He knows that in order to increase efficiency and profitability, a more prudent approach to new investments and the striving to ensure maximum exploitation of existing potential, i.e. of former investments, must be allied to an understanding of the need to plan consumption budgets so as to avoid financial complications in bad years and to save in good times.

This new approach to savings, not as an aim in itself but as a necessity for long-term stability, is one of the hallmarks of the new period. Within linear planning, each income-producing branch must be seen within the context of the whole economy, in which the concept of the "opportunity price" is very important. This means overcoming tendencies towards the "alienation" of the individual branch from the overall picture. These examples hint that the economic image of the kibbutz is changing: the whole operation is dependent on an up-to-the-moment system of cost accounting, but it is not only the accountant, the farm manager and the treasurer who have to work in this spirit. The branch manager must be equipped with the necessary know-how and understanding, but success depends not only upon the productive branches but no less on the consumption budgets. Unless these are co-related to the economic situation of the kibbutz at a given period, productivity will not necessarily mean profitability and the kibbutz will not be able to maintain sound financing of its overall functioning. This is the correct and logical way out of the kibbutz's financial difficulties and it is to be hoped that it will be adopted in a spirit of understanding by all concerned.

Though the kibbutz must pay its way like any commercial enterprise, the settlements were not established according to this criterion. They have to overcome the unfavourable economic circumstances in which they often work—poor soil, inadequate rainfall, high costs of water and for some settlements above all the heavy burden of security costs.

There are, too, some aspects of the kibbutz system as such which involve paying for the advantages it embodies for the members. To run a range of services, including education for all up to the age of 18 and complete care for the sick and aged in all circumstances, is an expensive proposition. It is hard to say whether the communal dining hall, with its bulk buying, is cheaper or more expensive than the private kitchen. In general, with about half the labour force working in various collective services in the kibbutz, the labour input in the family farm where the wife also helps out is much higher than in the kibbutz.

The kibbutzim did not always receive the financial aid customarily granted in Israel for the absorption of new immigrants in town and country. The older kibbutzim more than doubled their population since Statehood but in those founded between 1935–47,

3239 of the 8714 families received no budget at all and the remaining families got only 60 per cent of the budget. The great leap forward in the early years of the State was not soundly financed for the need was to absorb and feed the mass immigration at all costs. Afterwards there was an unfavourable relationship of agricultural prices to production costs and in 1960 farmers were earning 25 per cent less than the average of gainfully employed Jews.

In the years of wildfire growth, bad financing was overlooked or even encouraged by the Government because it lacked the resources needed to guarantee the financial consolidation of the settlements. This situation has changed meanwhile and there are some favourable pointers to be noted. One of the most important is the system of *directed settlements*—the financing by the Jewish Agency of those economic activities of a settlement confirmed by the Agency, in place of high interest commercial loans threatening the solvency of the settlement. At the same time, the Agency, in conjunction with the Federation to which the settlement belongs, helps to plan its economy and financing. Confirmation must be given to all new investment. In this way the finances of a kibbutz which has over-reached itself at a certain stage of its development and expansion are put in order and its economic activities are subjected to expert supervision.

Another constructive measure has been a series of conversion loans granted by the Government, Jewish Agency and *Histadrut*. These replaced some of the short-term, high-interest commercial loans with long-term, low-interest loans. Not all the kibbutzim found equal salvation in these measures. In 1966 about half the kibbutzim of the K.A. were paying from 5 to 10 per cent of their output in interest, a quarter were paying more than this and a quarter were paying less. The great differences between kibbutzim is reflected in the figures, which certainly show that many kibbutzim are still dangerously over-indebted.

Because it is mostly co-operative and collective, agriculture is the most planned and disciplined sectors of Israel's economy, far more amenable to planning than the largely privately owned industrial sector, for example. National planning is imperative and the kibbutz supports it to the hilt. However, if it penalises agriculture or the kibbutz within agriculture—and there have been examples of both—it can have the most dangerous consequences. Such planning, in short, cannot be divorced from the socio-economic trends underlying it, from the image of the regime at which it aims.

Much has been done since the days of austerity and the surplus crisis to enable the efficient farmer to make an honourable living. Yet that there is a long way to go is shown in the fact that in 1966 prices of agricultural output rose 3·5 per cent, of input by 5·5 per cent. These are conditions which make profitability unlikely, even with high productivity.

In Israel's economy it is overall government policy which determines the economic status of the various sectors, and not least of agriculture. The Government not only fixes prices but it is also the decisive factor in determining the relation of prices to production costs through all the ramifications of its credit policy, interest rates, subsidies, import and export duties, middlemen's profits, etc. To a major degree, government policy is therefore decisive in creating, or not creating, the conditions in which agriculture can enjoy its fair chance of reaching a profitability commensurate with its productivity.

After a generation of pioneering work, the aim should surely be to enable the kibbutz to become an enterprise with a healthy basis of its own capital. Not only are the demands of the kibbutz compatible with the interests of the economy: they are a precondition for its correct development—for without a stable and rooted farming population the whole structure is unsound. Credit facilities, the raising of the purchasing power of the poorer sections of the population, assurances that the farmer's standard of income will not fall behind that of other sectors—these are good for the kibbutz but not only for the kibbutz. They are an essential part of a sound economic policy for the whole country.

To sum up, we can see that the economic future of the kibbutz depends not only on its own ability to exploit the inherent advantages of its own socio-economic structure but also upon the economic, political and social stresses to which it is subjected. Some important factors are within its control—increasing productivity without overreaching in investment, correct planning of consumption budgets, etc. But fundamentally, its prospects are inseparable from developments from within the environment in which it operates. If it is comparable to a fortress consolidating its own defences and at the same time fighting against would-be destroyers, such a situation demands both internal economic initiative and a political offensive to make its influence felt outside its home territory.

This offensive would be inconceivable without the economic power which the kibbutz has won for itself. In this, the Kibbutz Artzi has played a worthy role and no special purpose would be served by singling out its contribution in a field where many, though not all, the basic assumptions are common to the whole kibbutz movement.

Unfortunately, the same cannot always be said as regards the relationship of the kibbutz to the society surrounding it. Only time can tell whether the increasing co-operation between the kibbutz movements in the economic sphere will be accompanied by a growing understanding of a truth which the Kibbutz Artzi has never for a moment overlooked: that even the strongest fortress is pregnable if it fails to reach a correct evaluation of the forces lined up against it.

CHAPTER 4

Kibbutz Democracy

THE first communes, numbering less than twenty young men and women, applied the most direct democratic method in order to make decisions. After the day's work, they would sit down together, thrash out all their problems, small and large, and decide what work had to be done, who would do it, and how the meagre resources of the group would be allocated. This was a most natural development, for one of the sources of the commune was the revolt of the settlers against taking orders from an appointed manager, who symbolised the system of external bureaucratic control and internal social differentiation.

THEN AND NOW

This was all very well as long as the commune resembled an enlarged family group. As it grew, and as its economic and social life took on new dimensions of size and complexity, its democratic management became far more complicated and problematical. Nevertheless, the kibbutz remains so democratic that observers often ask whether its principles of democratic management do not impair efficiency, and how its fight against bureaucracy is compatible with that authority to make decisions and execute them effectively without which it would be impotent.

The founders of the Kibbutz Artzi spoke of the kibbutz as an *organic unit*. In this phrase, they expressed their opposition to the very small family-like group on the one hand, and on the other hand to the conception that there were no limits to the potential numerical growth of a kibbutz. However, the essence of the organic kibbutz is not only in its numerical framework, but also in the relationship between its various functions and of the members to each other and to these functions. In other words, *the organic functioning of the kibbutz depends upon its internal cohesion, upon the degree of consciousness and identification with the group of its members, and upon the correct balance between the varied functions* which the group is called upon to carry out. The only guarantee for the realisation of this organic development is in the *maximum democratisation* of kibbutz life at all levels and in all spheres.

How, then, does kibbutz democracy work out in practice, and what are its major problems?

THE MEMBERS' MEETING

The highest forum of kibbutz democracy is the members' meeting, or general assembly, which meets about once a week and has been compared to the parliament of the kibbutz. The authority of the members' meeting is unlimited both in its scope and in its powers of decision: it can—and does—discuss and resolve not only major policy questions in all spheres, but it also has jurisdiction over less vital matters which an individual, or a committee, wishes to bring before it. In this forum new members are accepted, office-holders and committees are elected, annual and short-term economic, financial and manpower plans are accepted, and all the social, educational, ideological and cultural questions of kibbutz life are resolved through the discussion of current problems and the clarification of basic issues and principles.

The agenda of the general assembly is as broad and varied as kibbutz life itself, and just as every member has the right to express his point of view and to vote, so the democratic decision of the assembly is binding upon the whole membership. All decisions are taken by an open majority vote, though some categories demand a minimum vote and/or a two-thirds majority. Over the years, the forms regulating the conduct of the meeting have crystallised to the point where a fairly extensive written and unwritten procedure now exists. This covers such questions as the right of a member or a committee to appeal against a decision, the ways in which a member can ensure that a matter of importance is included on the agenda, the obligations of those responsible for various committees to report on their activities, and the dividing-line between matters which demand confirmation by the meeting and those in which this is unnecessary.

There are, of course, some very personal and intimate questions which can only be resolved in smaller forums than the members' meeting in order to spare embarrassing a particular member. However, these are comparatively few. Week by week, the members' meeting is the scene of heated discussion and controversy. Each point on the agenda, which has been announced on the notice-board before the meeting, is introduced by the Secretary or the member responsible for the matter under discussion. A simple issue might be resolved quickly, but the discussion is frequently prolonged over more than one meeting.

Finally, the Secretariat's proposals (possibly revised in light of the discussion) are put to the vote. If, as often happens, they are rejected, members may put to the vote alternative resolutions. Appeals are often made against decisions, but once a matter is finally resolved in the members' meeting, the decision must be carried out, even if the Secretariat, or the appropriate committee, is of a different opinion.

It would be hard to give a "typical" agenda, for this varies enormously, and there is no limit to the questions, old and new, which must be resolved. Here is a random sample of the agenda in my own kibbutz during two weeks: Building programme, financial report, acceptance of a new candidate, a request to visit parents abroad, election of the Appointments Committee, a movement request to release a member for educational work. Incidentally, most of these topics were debated at some length, and two of them, the first and the last, were carried over to subsequent meetings.

THE SECRETARIAT

If the general assembly is comparable to the Parliament, the Secretariat is comparable to the kibbutz "Cabinet". It must be small enough to assure its efficiency as an executive body; yet its composition must be sufficiently broad to ensure that it represents the various functions whose internal "balance" is, as we have seen, of such decisive importance for the functioning of the whole system. The Secretariat must therefore include the three or four members currently occupying the central offices* of farm-manager, secretary, treasurer, and work-organiser. Most kibbutzim also include on the Secretariat the chairmen, or representatives of, the education and social committees, and of the youth section in older settlements.

The Secretariat is responsible to the general assembly for the whole of the kibbutz administration. It supervises the work of all the committees. As such, it executes policies decided upon by the assembly, and exercises decisive control over the whole functioning of the kibbutz. It would be hard to exaggerate the extent to which its internal cohesion, initiative, understanding and efficiency regulate the tempo of kibbutz progress in all fields. It must work as a team and accept collective responsibility for hundreds of large and small decisions. Though it is always subject to decisions of the members' meeting, it can do much to direct public opinion, to mobilise the kibbutz for priority action in one sector or another. It formulates the agenda for the members' meeting, and though the latter may reject its proposals, no other body can be compared to the secretariat in terms of its possibilities of influencing public opinion.

Since the Secretariat is so representative, it has at its disposal such comprehensive expert knowledge that its proposals have special authority in the eyes of all members, few of whom have the same chance to weigh up the many factors involved in policy-making in an organisation as complex as the kibbutz. This is one of the reasons why the balanced functioning of the kibbutz as a whole depends so much on the Secretariat, whose concentration of authority is subordinate only to the members' meeting. Indeed, the relationship between these two forums and their mutual confidence

---

* It is somewhat misleading to translate the Hebrew "*Baal-tafkid*", literally task-holder, as functionary or even official. Both words smack of bureaucracy, while all tasks in the kibbutz are rotated so that the "senior official" of today may be an ordinary worker tomorrow.

—or lack of it—is one of the dominant aspects of democratic management in the kibbutz.

COMMITTEES

In the scale of kibbutz democracy, a wide range of committees play an important role. Unlike the general assembly or the Secretariat, they are restricted in their functions to a special area for which they are responsible to the latter bodies. Every area of kibbutz life is supervised by the appropriate committee. Separate committees (sometimes functioning through sub-committees) deal with economic matters, manpower, social affairs, education, culture, festivals, adult education, the kibbutz bulletin, political activity, security, health, absorption of newcomers, sport, etc. Special committees are often elected for specific purposes. In addition, an appointments committee brings suggestions to the general assembly for the composition of the kibbutz administration at the annual elections.

The committees, whose membership is usually about five or six (though it can be smaller or larger in some cases) are elected for a year, but a degree of continuity is assured by leaving one or two members of the old committee on a new elected body. Each committee has its chairman, and usually divides the area for which it is responsible into sub-areas, with which one or two members deal. If a committee is dynamic, well-organised and fundamental in its work, its impact is felt everywhere in the kibbutz; if it does its job superficially and haphazardly, this is no less felt by the members.

Committee work not only prepares members for central tasks: it encompasses over 50 per cent of the kibbutz membership year by year and thereby assures that the feeling of members that the kibbutz is theirs, and that they run it, finds concrete expression. It does away with the distinction between those who decide and those for whom others decide. It prevents the development of an inactive periphery, and channelises the creative inclinations of members—which might otherwise be stifled—into the major stream of kibbutz activity.

However, the committees are not artificially created bodies whose aim is to activise the members. On the contrary, the all-round functioning of the kibbutz would be impossible without the effective work they do. The organisation of the cultural life of a kibbutz, for example, is a task so considerable that it demands the most serious attention and study, organisation and initiative, individual and collective ability. A successful cultural committee enriches the life of the whole kibbutz membership, and an unsuccessful committee condemns the kibbutz to a boring and colourless spiritual life. The same is true in other areas. The success or failure of the committees does much to determine the whole character, direction and intensity of kibbutz life. In a sense, it would be true to say that committee work is the measuring-board of the ability of the kibbutz to run its affairs properly, and, as such, it is easy to understand the extent to which this influences the satisfaction and happiness of the whole membership.

WORK-BRANCH DEMOCRACY

We have already referred to the fourth rung in the scale of kibbutz democracy—the team of workers in a particular branch or service (see p. 41). Since a large part of the day is occupied with work, and most kibbutz members are more or less permanently occupied in their branch, its democratic management is a question of increasing importance, especially as the kibbutz grows and different generations meet in the fields, at the factory bench, or in the services. There is a good deal to be said for the view that the increasing attention now given to this subject is an expression of the need to add a new dimension to kibbutz democracy in view of the demographic changes through which the older settlements are passing as they become less homogeneous.

Kibbutz reality is, first and foremost, that of people working together. A new generation, or a youth group from Israel or abroad, sees in its workmates the most concrete expression of a group of people pooling their human resources in a co-operative effort to achieve clearly-defined common aims. In this sense, democratic management in the kibbutz starts in the branch, no less than in a committee or in the general assembly. The problems of the branch occupy its workers for 8 hours a day at least. If, therefore, they are not democratically resolved, an important dimension of kibbutz democracy would be missing. The branch-organiser is not a foreman giving orders to subordinates, but a comrade leading a team of equals. All this helps to explain why human relations within the branch, and its democratic running, are taking on increasing importance as kibbutz society searches for more, and more effective, expressions of its democratic content.

It would probably be hard to find a more democratic framework in the world than the kibbutz, not so much because of its formal democratic structure, but rather because of the egalitarian social content with which this is filled. We know, in fact, that a democratic constitution is no guarantee of genuinely democratic processes. In modern society there are forces at work—such as the alienation of the individual and his feeling of impotence in the face of technocracy and bureaucracy—which provide a fertile breeding-ground for apathy, for the feeling that the individual counts for little, and has no real power to determine the destiny of his society.

The large kibbutz framework which we know today, with its many highly complicated functions and its heterogeneous composition, cannot expect to be automatically immune to these trends. (Paradoxical as it may sound, both ancient and recent history know of authoritarian communes and bureaucratic Socialism.) Kibbutz democracy faces problems of its own which it would be folly to overlook, and this notwithstanding such "built-in" brakes to anti-democratic trends as social equality and the mass participation of nearly all the members in kibbutz administration.

ACTIVISATION OF MEMBERS

Though it is almost impossible to live kibbutz life without a reasonable level of general identification with the commune, its degree may vary considerably, depending on a variety of objective and subjective factors, including individual character and inclination.

There is always a certain "periphery" in the kibbutz which, for one reason or another, takes insufficient interest in its public affairs, is reluctant to work in a committee, and, unlike the majority of members, does not even participate in the weekly members' meeting. Incidentally, such people may, paradoxically, be exemplary workers, which indicates how involved are the matters under discussion.

The kibbutz has at its disposal a wealth of possibilities for the activisation of its members, and this is indeed one of the main tasks of the appointments committee, of other committees, and of the Secretariat. But there is a point of view, and it is not completely without foundation, that as the kibbutz grows numerically, as its population becomes more varied, and as the vital problems which face it in all facets of life become more complex and demand more specialised knowledge, so the members' meeting becomes less able to fulfil its correct role in kibbutz democracy. Some see a tendency towards the exaggerated delegation of its powers to smaller and more "competent" forums like the Secretariat, the appropriate committee, or even an individual member particularly experienced in the matter under discussion.

The same tendency may explain not only why some members do not attend the general meeting, but also how it happens that important decisions may be made by the votes of a comparatively small percentage of those present. Some abstain out of a feeling that without expert knowledge, it is impossible to choose between alternative suggestions; others do so for a host of other reasons, such as a certain reluctance to take sides, for points of view are represented in the kibbutz not by anonymous officials from outside but by men and women whose lives are bound together and interrelated in every sphere.

INTEREST GROUPS

Neither is the kibbutz immune to the development of *interest groups* whose specific interests are not necessarily identical with those of the community. The education committee knows that if it suggests a suitable candidate for work with a particular group of children, it is assured the votes of their parents. But in order to take up educational work, she must give up the important work she is doing in the poultry branch, and a "counter-lobby" of branch workers might vote against the suggestion. Such "lobbies" can develop in every area of kibbutz life, based upon the particular interests and inclinations of workers in a branch or service, of the members of a similar age-group demanding a decision about the building programme which serves their special needs, or of a committee fighting for a bigger financial allocation.

But these random examples—which could be multiplied tenfold —also hint at forces working in the opposite direction. For the worker in a certain branch is also a parent, and the chairman of the education committee may be working in the poultry branch! In so far as there are interest groups, they are very rarely permanent, and kibbutz life is so dynamic and mobile, its many functions so interdependent, that the subjective "interests" of the member are not comparable to those which are endemic in class societies. Furthermore, the selective nature of kibbutz society, the high educational standards both of the founders and of the new generation, the degree of identification with the commune (usually called "idealism" by outside observers), and a certain unwritten code of ethics without which the kibbutz would disintegrate—all these make it difficult to compare "voting habits" in the general assembly with similar forums elsewhere. The kibbutz has what may be called a *collective conscience* and it is frequently this which determines decisions no less than other, and more negative, considerations.

NO BUREAUCRACY!

Even so, those studying kibbutz administration and searching for ways to activise the members and to deepen its democratic content are aware of the magnitude of their task. They point to the pressing need to streamline the channels of communication between the commune and its members, to provide information on its complicated operation in forms understandable to all, so that economic and financial problems, for example, will not become the specialised province of a few experts. Learning from the outside world, as well as from kibbutz experience, they stress that teamwork is more effective than bossism and that the most effective organisation is dependent for its success upon "informal" human relations.

The rotation of tasks, facilitated by a broad and increasing network of study courses for those holding office in the kibbutz, would appear to secure the kibbutz against the public enemy number one of democracy—bureaucracy. Both those in office today, and those who will be in office tomorrow, know that unless they find a common language of understanding, temporary victories of prestige, or of sectional interests, or the exploitation of an official task to settle a private feud, cannot—as in class societies—bring positive rewards, material or otherwise. For prestige in the kibbutz is won not by steamroller tactics and ruthlessness in personal relations, but by the extent to which a member brings to his task human understanding as well as devotion and organisational ability.

Indeed, most kibbutz members prefer to avoid the tensions and responsibilities of the four or five tasks which are considered to be the most important in what others call the "hierarchy" of management. Very often these central offices are not filled without extended and exhaustive negotiation and persuasion, culminating in the vote of the members' meeting. In the last analysis, the discipline of the collective almost invariably prevails, but only the naïve will fail to understand that the clashes occurring from time to time between the inclinations of the individual and the needs of the collective in many areas of kibbutz life give birth to grave social and individual problems. This is why kibbutz management requires not only efficient organisation but also genuine insight and the realisation that, in the kibbutz far more than elsewhere, it is the human factor which is often decisive in the ultimate reckoning.

INDIVIDUAL AND COMMUNITY

The real enemy of kibbutz democracy would not appear to be bureaucracy, and neither would it appear to be true that the rotation of tasks is necessarily at the expense of efficiency, as long as the training facilities for such specialised offices as farm manager* are systematically exploited, so that the circle of members with expert knowledge in this and other fields can constantly grow. Far more dangerous is the tendency in the large kibbutz for the centrifugal forces within the kibbutz to grow and for the individual to be so occupied with his own work, his own family, his own social circle and his own interests that he loses sight of the organic totality of kibbutz life. This is one of the most serious expressions of the inability to see the wood for the trees.

We have hinted at some of the ways in which this tendency can be combatted. Better organisation, better planning of human resources, better channels of communication and better training for various offices can do much to alleviate the problem. But there is no substitute in the kibbutz for the type of overall identification which has its roots in the ideological consciousness of the individual. This is what builds and fortifies the collective will and integrates the individual with the whole of the commune rather than with one aspect of its life. This is the source from which all the streams and channels of kibbutz democracy flow and without which they would run dry. And as the kibbutz grows, there can be no doubt that constant study and work will have to be invested in order to ensure that the source is deep enough and the channels wide enough to carry the democratisation of kibbutz life forward from stage to stage.

* After studying for about a year, a member may occupy this position for as long as three years. Accountancy is a profession and not a rotating office. Experts in a special area may be re-elected after a break in office, during which they can still sit in the appropriate committee.

CHAPTER 5

Equality and Incentives

IN CLASS society, talk of "equal rights" and "equal opportunity" is either empty phraseology or it refers to possibilities within strictly limited confines, for economic inequality, between classes and within them, is the ultimate factor determining what the individual gives to, and receives from, society. Historically speaking, the Soviet Union is, from an economic point of view in what Marx called "the first phase of communist society, when it has just emerged, after prolonged birth-pangs, from capitalist society".

Marx has explained the development of communist society, which, at first, is compelled to abolish only the "injustice" of the means of production having been seized by private individuals. It cannot immediately abolish the other injustice of the distribution of consumer articles "according to the amount of work performed" and not according to needs.*

In this respect, the kibbutz represents the higher stage of "from each according to his ability, to each according to his needs"; though one must add the reservation—according to the possibilities of the commune. We must not forget, of course, that the kibbutz

---

* The original formulation of Marx (in his *Critique of the Gotha Programme*) reads: "Only at a higher stage of communist society, after the abolition of the enslavement of the individual to the division of labour and the distinction between mental and physical labour; after labour will have become not merely a means of existence, but the prime necessity of life; after the means of production will have grown together with the all-round development of the individual, and all sources of social wealth will be flowing richer—only then can the narrow horizon of bourgeois justice be left behind and society will be able to inscribe on its banners: from each according to his ability—to each according to his needs."

is a small and selective society, and far from the achievement of material abundance, but equality certainly exists in all the basic spheres of kibbutz life—work, food, housing, education, the care for the sick, etc.*

RIGHTS AND OBLIGATIONS

The kibbutz knows no constitutional definition of the rights and obligations of its members. Human beings are never exactly equal in ambition or ability, and in the commune no machinery of coercion or punishment compels them to act, or not to act, in a particular fashion. What, then, are the motive forces behind the kibbutz as a voluntary society in which none of the accepted incentives of personal wealth and progress, of direct material remuneration for more or better work, would seem to apply?

There is no single answer and no easy answer to the question. It is true that the kibbutz is a highly selective society, but the sort of idealisation which permeates a novel like *Exodus* by Leon Uris probably does more to distort the issues than to clarify them. Idealism and idealisation are very different things indeed, and those who would see the kibbutz as a haven for heroes are about as wide of the mark as those who see it as a refuge for social cases. What is true is that people's motivation is influenced by the values of their society, which play an important role in determining how the potential of the individual is developed and for what reasons.

---

* It is interesting to note that when a Soviet theoretician, Academician Strumilin, poses the question of what form life in his country will take once Communism has been achieved, his reflections about the commune which he envisages as rising in ten or twenty years are surprisingly close in many aspects to kibbutz life. The family, freed of its economic functions, will be based solely on the love and friendship of its two partners. There will be communal education, directed by suitably qualified educators, from infancy to maturity, and communal houses, in which each family will have its own modest apartment, with communal services: dining-rooms, laundries, etc. He proposes the early establishment of communes which can serve as models and pilot plants for the study of the problems involved in this type of living. As for "the reality of human relations" in the Soviet Union see p. 92. Sartre's comment (see p. 25) is most relevant here!

Even so, there is no single incentive motivating the kibbutz. Since people are different, it would seem natural that different incentives influence different types of people. Though the kibbutz as a society has a very special sense of purpose, it would be absurd to say that, except in times of crisis or emergency, the whole population goes about its daily work with a conscious feeling of inspiration, elation, and sense of belonging to a better society. Without its "collective conscience", the kibbutz is unthinkable, but if pure altruism were its only motivation, it could hardly have reached its present dimensions and achievements.

Public opinion in the kibbutz is undoubtedly a powerful incentive. The kibbutz is small enough to harbour few secrets, and among people who live so close to each other it is almost impossible for a member to live in the community without pulling his weight at work. The atmosphere of hard work makes lead-swinging or loafing unusually impossible. Public opinion, which can be indulgent towards many human weaknesses, is so intolerant of idling that it will make life intolerable for anyone who would like to benefit from the hard-won privileges of kibbutz membership without accepting its most basic obligation—hard work.

It is this atmosphere which also encourages initiative at work and leads to lively competition between individuals, between branches and between settlements. Nothing is more highly valued by public opinion than "a good worker" and an outstanding worker is proportionally respected—indeed it is doubtful whether any other single factor is more important in determining the respect in which people are held. We have already noted that the kibbutz has led Jewish agriculture for some three decades in progress and innovations, and in the annual work-prizes which are a feature of Israeli life the kibbutzim are always prominent. This is not the result of bureaucratic administrative compulsions, but of the conscious effort of the individual and of the branch in which he works.

PRESTIGE

Outside the kibbutz, prestige and social differentiation are often inseparable, but within it one cannot keep up with the Joneses by showing off a bigger house or a more expensive car. Because there are no differences in material levels, prestige depends so much on the individual's record at work. This is one of the ways in which the ambition to do well, to get on, to be respected, to gain status—call it what you will—finds its expression in the kibbutz framework, and public opinion is just as appreciative of devotion to work, of efficiency and of successful results as it is intolerant of the opposite.

The average kibbutz member, who can neither be fired nor expropriated from his land, needs no more "supervision" in his work than a private farmer working his own land. A kibbutz shepherd will speak of "my flock". He feels the whole farm is "ours" and his special branch is "mine"—and towards the latter he has a special sense of responsibility. But though material incentives are collective and not personal, they undoubtedly have great importance in determining the kibbutz member's attitude to work. He knows that the standard of living and the social security of him and his family depend upon the income of the farm and factory and that this depends upon his efforts—though not only on his efforts. Along with others, he feels the obligation not only to pay his passage, so to speak, but also to raise his own standards through his own contribution to the general effort.

MOTIVATION AND SATISFACTION

This by no means implies that everyone is equally satisfied with his work, for it is natural to prefer interesting to boring work, a skilled job to unskilled labour and so on. People are more or less compatible to agricultural work and to physical labour in general, and some may find the choice of jobs limited and frustrating. Not all the criteria we have mentioned have the same applicability to the services as to work in agriculture or industry. Though loafers have no place in the kibbutz, people in the commune, like those outside, tend to be more or less industrious or lazy, ambitious or unambitious, organised or haphazard, creative or passive, conscientious or careless in their work.

Many people in the kibbutz, like skilled workers or craftsmen elsewhere, feel such a sense of pride in their work that to do the job properly is an end in itself, an expression of that creative urge upon which Socialist ethics are founded. They might find it hard to explain their motivations, since they find their satisfaction in the actual process and result of their labour, and the idea of turning out a shoddy piece of work, or going slow when the foreman's back is turned, never occurs to them. Such people, deeply attached to their place of work and proud of their contribution to its progress, provide the ultimate answer to cynics who deny that men and women are capable of "voluntarily working according to their ability".

Different incentives, therefore, motivate different people. There are people in the kibbutz who are satisfied to pull their weight without over-exerting themselves, but who knows whether the incentives of competitive society could develop their potential more effectively? These are imponderables rooted in the different psychological make-up of human beings: in general, we can sum up that the kibbutz system not only works, but serves to encourage a type of devotion to work and creative initiative the like of which it would be hard to find elsewhere in Israel, or outside it.

FIG. 1. Monument to the heroic defenders of Kibbutz Negba during
the War of Independence.

Fig. 2. The beginnings of Kibbutz Beit Alfa, first kibbutz of the Kibbutz Artzi, which was established in 1922.

Fig. 3. General view of veteran kibbutz today.

FIG. 4. Farm buildings, including modern poultry house, in veteran kibbutz. (Moshe Lapidot [Mizra].)

FIG. 5. Pruning. (Moshe Lapidot [Mizra].)

FIG. 6. In the cotton fields. (David Perlmutter [Kfar Menachem].)

FIG. 7. A kibbutz factory producing ply-wood boxes. (Moshe Lapidot [Mizra].)

FIG. 8. Modern dining-hall in an older kibbutz. (Moshe Lapidot [Mizra].)

FIG. 9. Weekly members' meeting in kibbutz dining-hall. (Mordechai Abrahamov [Yakum].)

Fig. 10. Relaxing in the evening in kibbutz club-room. (*Moadon le' chaver.*)

Fig. 11. Kibbutz Festival. (Moshe Lapidot [Mizraj.)

FIG. 12. Celebrating the harvest festival.

FIG. 13. In a kibbutz primary school.

FIG. 14. In the toddlers' house. (Moshe Lapidot [Mizra].)

Fig. 15. Kibbutz youth orchestra rehearsing.

Fig. 16. Examining the damage after the shelling of the crèche in a "border incident". The children of this kibbutz had been taken to the shelters before the attack. (Moshe Lapidot [Mizra].)

Fig. 17. After the Six-Day War of 1967: how the kibbutizm Dan and Dafne looked from the Syrian positions dominating them from above. The settlements were constantly harassed from here until the positions were taken by the Israelis during the war.

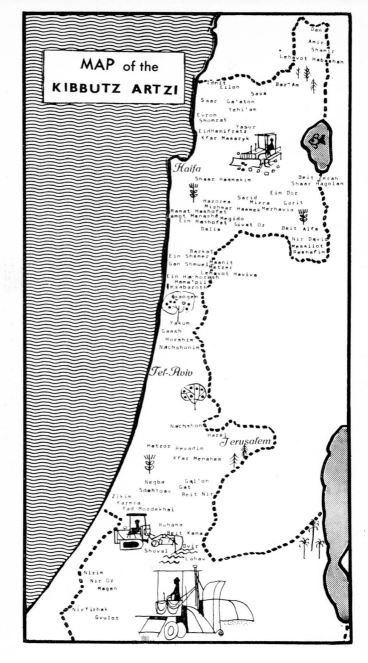

FIG. 18. Map of the Kibbutz Artizi (1967)

CHAPTER 6

Collective Consumption:
The Individual and the Commune

Two principles dominate the practice of collective consumption in the kibbutz. It must provide for all the needs of the population, which are determined collectively, and there must be equal distribution regardless of what type of work the member is doing. Collective consumption encompasses all the major and minor needs of the individual and of the family—food, housing, education, clothing, medical care, culture and entertainment, pocket money, vacations, full social security in illness and old age,* and an endless list of less important items ranging from postage stamps to razor blades and from hairpins to running repairs on the house.

PROVIDING AND DISTRIBUTING

Since the list of needs in modern life is without end, it would be pointless to try and detail them, but it is essential to understand that in the kibbutz there is no connection whatsoever between the work a member and his wife are doing and the house they live in or the education their children receive. Naturally, a teacher requires different clothes from a mechanic, and a pregnant woman, or a man on a diet, requires special food. Equality does not mean standardisation and it cannot be mechanical, but it rules out different standards of living based upon any of the criteria which determine this elsewhere.

* Social security in the kibbutz is complete and unlimited in duration. This applies not only to the member but also to his parents, many of whom live in the kibbutz as of right or are helped to live outside by the kibbutz.

The expenses incurred in the maintenance of each member only vary according to varying needs, such as the number of children or dependents. The kibbutz must decide upon a lump sum for each area of consumption, broken down in order to cover as far as possible the whole of the kibbutz needs; this represents the consumption outlay of the whole settlement. The overall budget of the kibbutz is determined by a whole series of decisions on needs and priorities between the productive sector (the running expenses of branches, maintenance, farm building, amortisation, investment, etc.) and the non-productive sector. All these must be balanced within a financial framework dictated by the position of the kibbutz economy at any given time. Only within these limits can the consumption budget try to meet the needs of the kibbutz population.

Accordingly, there are very considerable differences in the standard of living in kibbutzim, and especially between young and veteran settlements. Serious attention is being given by the Kibbutz Artzi to strengthening already existing measures, such as internal movement taxation and mutual aid, which aim to narrow this gap. For though each kibbutz enjoys a degree of autonomy in determining internal priorities, the extent of central movement intervention and supervision of the budget is infinitely greater than is generally known. Norms are laid down for expenditure in every sector, and though a kibbutz may prefer to spend more on one item in the budget at a particular stage at the expense of another, economic realities and movement discipline all limit the bounds in which most kibbutzim can manoeuvre.

SYSTEMS OF DISTRIBUTION

It would be impossible to apply the principles of equality in the field of consumption through the use of a standard allocation system, so, in practice, different criteria are employed for different commodities and services, as the following examples will show.

Working-clothes, toilet requisites, cleaning materials and cigarettes are allocated literally according to need, virtually without restriction.

Clothes belong to individuals, for the time has long passed when it was considered "bourgeois" to own a garment or to dress attractively after work. Unlike working-clothes and boots, which are simply replaced when they wear out, as the system evolved it was generally found more satisfactory to allocate according to a quota system based on norms worked out by the Kibbutz Artzi. Thus a member was entitled to receive so many shirts, dresses, etc., per year, with the norms taking into account all the types of garment, footwear and linens which the kibbutz decides to include in the budget, and the wear and tear of each of them. Lately this system has been modified to cater for personal choice. When the kibbutz member furnishes his room, he can, of course, buy his curtains, carpets and so on according to his choice within a certain price range.

For housing and basic furniture an entirely different system is necessary, for kibbutz housing ranges from comfortable two-roomed flats with toilet and showers for older members to quite primitive wooden huts with communal showers and toilets for younger people. In the Kibbutz Artzi, for want of a more equitable method of deciding how to allocate housing, a points system determines who will live where. It is reckoned according to length of membership (3 points per year) and age (a point for every year between 18 and 40, and 2 points per year from the age of 40 onwards).

The question of food presents no special problems as regards allocation, since the three main meals are eaten in the communal dining-hall where the menu is fairly varied and special diets, of course, catered for. (The problem of satisfying different tastes is more complicated, and not everyone is always satisfied with the menu!) Each house has a small kitchenette with simple cooking facilities, so that anyone wishing to take food home and prepare it may do so. However, members usually do this only on special occasions, except for afternoon tea which the family regularly takes at home with the children.

LIVING STANDARDS

Theoretically, the kibbutz is able to determine its living standards autonomously and simply to raise or lower budgets according to the financial situation at a given time. In practice, this is a highly complicated issue, for the standard of living in Israel has been consistently rising for years and the kibbutz cannot divorce itself completely from outside trends. Though it started as a "commune of poverty", this was never an ideology in the Kibbutz Artzi, and the kibbutz aims to provide a decent standard of living for its members.

To take housing as an example, the most expensive kibbutz house is built according to modest specifications and furnished comfortably but by no means luxuriously. Until the kibbutz can provide them with even a one-room flat, members live in the most primitive conditions, for the whole housing situation in the kibbutz lags far behind city standards. It is not easy to urge further austerity on hard-working men and women who know that people of the same age who came to Israel with them on the same boat have enjoyed decent accommodation in town for years.

An additional problem is that if the kibbutz were to stop building in bad years, the sacrifice involved would not, as in a family, be equally divided, for a certain sector of the population which is in line for permanent housing would suffer, while those already living in decent accommodation would not feel the pinch at all. A similar difficulty exists in education and elsewhere. All this hints how hard it is to cut down living standards in times of financial stress and why this touchy subject is often the cause of stormy controversy in the committees and general assembly which draw up the annual budget.

In spite of the difficulties, the standard of living and consumption budgets are of necessity based upon financial realities, for productive investment receives priority and a policy of piling up short-term loans at exorbitant rates of interest can only result in increasing financial complications. For many years the kibbutzim had therefore to put up with ramshackle, under-equipped and inadequate dining-halls, delaying the construction of the new, modern and efficient kitchens and dining-halls so necessary for their growing population. The tempo of building for members and children is cut down in bad times, vacations are cut out and other points in the consumption budget pegged or cut back.

In dealing with the kibbutz economy we noted the difficulties involved in comparing overall living standards of the kibbutz with town or moshav. Different ways of life involve different consumption habits, possibilities, priorities and expectations. There is also the problem of how to make valid comparative calculations. Whereas the urban worker with a steady job may spend more in good times, he lacks the unprecedented social security which the kibbutz family enjoys under all circumstances. The latter takes for granted secondary education for every kibbutz child, an expensive item for town dwellers. On the other hand, the kibbutz family may feel it has shorter or more limited vacation facilities and young people that they have less chance for university study.

In general, kibbutz standards of living are comparable to those of skilled workers in the city. Between 1962 and 1965 the real rise of living standards in the kibbutz was similar to that in Israel as a whole (6–7 per cent). E. Kanowskÿ notes that "in 1962 consumption standards in the kibbutzim were approximately 5–10 per cent below those of the average Jewish urban family and probably more than 25 per cent below those of the established European and American immigrants" (with whom, incidentally, the kibbutz member will compare himself).

Nevertheless, one cannot altogether discount the criticism of those who express the view that there is insufficient attunement between income and spending by the kibbutz since consumption norms recommended by the Federation are to some extent isolated from economic achievements or failures in a given year. Though much progress has been made in study courses, building and other aspects of the services, planning of consumption certainly lags behind planning of production in the kibbutz. Whereas the planning of production is founded on obvious criteria like profitability, this is not so in consumption. Taking the dining-hall as an example, even granted the most modern equipment and work methods in the kitchen as well as financial competence in purchasing foodstuffs, there is no guarantee that the kibbutz members will be satisfied with the set-up. This is because the real purpose of kitchen and other services is to satisfy individual needs and tastes and not only to run a sound economic operation.

Tastes vary and the aim is to satisfy everyone; gone are the days when all had to put up with the lowest (cheapest) common denominator. However, may there not be a danger of going towards the opposite extreme and fixing the most expensive taste as a new common denominator in the "commune of plenty"? Further, to fix priorities in the consumption budget may be harder than in production because it will be tougher to resist pressures from interested groups—for example, from those pressing for better housing, further studies or trips abroad. Such pressures, with their social implications, can make it hard to stick to the budget as planned without causing dissatisfaction to one party or the other. In this case, to honour the kibbutz principle of trying to satisfy the members may come at the expense of sound financial policy.

The various methods of regulating living standards are unpopular and undertaken reluctantly. Yet the sense of responsibility of the general assembly which must decide upon them very rarely fails, and the central movement institutions can intervene in order to compel a kibbutz struggling with these problems to face up to realities and avoid exaggerated spending in bad years.

EQUALITY—YES, STANDARDISATION—NO!

Among the problems of collective consumption, the kibbutz is no less aware than its critics that decisive importance is attached to the satisfaction of individual choice and taste. In backward societies and in times of austerity, people are satisfied merely to receive, but the more advanced the person and the more advanced the society, the more important becomes the question: is what I have received really what I want? In the so-called "affluent" capitalist society, people may be persuaded to want things they do not even need, for reasons of status and prestige. In the kibbutz the question is quite different, for we are speaking of the real needs of cultured and conscious people (who are influenced by consumption habits outside, but certainly not for prestige reasons).

Mechanical equality is neither just nor equal, for equality without choice satisfied none of those who are meant to be equal—unless they are robots rather than human beings with different tastes, inclinations, interests and potential. People in the kibbutz want to be equal, but not the same, so that over-standardisation and real equality have little in common. Genuine equality and reasonable freedom of choice go together, but we are referring to genuine freedom, which has nothing to do with television commercials and the whole gigantic apparatus which in some of the self-styled "free countries" assure freedom of profit by smothering good taste and the real freedom of the individual to choose, under the blanket of conformism and commercialism.

There is no evidence that collective consumption, as such, cannot cater for individual tastes or that freedom of choice is incompatible with equality. But as the kibbutz is able to provide more for its members, it must prove this not only objectively, but also subjectively, and the two do not always go hand in hand.

It is true that in some areas this is more difficult than in others, for it is not easy for a cook to cater for the individual tastes of hundreds of people. But there is no reason whatsoever why there should be standardisation in clothes or furniture chosen within a certain price range. It is the norms which are standard and not the trousers.

However, this depends upon the correct organisation of the clothes-store and the flexible approach of the member responsible for it. Unless she is prepared to go to the trouble of ordering a large choice, or of enabling a member who is not satisfied with the choice to buy outside, then dissatisfaction is inevitable. The same applies to most commodities: the kibbutz system is capable of catering for individual tastes, and increasing efforts are now being devoted to streamlining organisation and training the people in charge. The atmosphere in the clothes-store can be cold, impersonal and bureaucratic, or friendly and understanding of different tastes. These are the factors which determine the attitude of members, and they depend on how the system is operated, rather than on the system itself.

THE THIN END OF THE WEDGE

Collective consumption is a revolutionary concept in which the kibbutz can learn little from outside, for in a co-operative framework like the kolkhoz, collectivity is only applied to production. The kibbutz is extraordinarily sensitive in this area to outside influences —to the infiltration of alien tendencies which, however worthy their intentions, could lead to the transformation of the kibbutz into a co-operative* instead of a collective, by undermining its internal equality.

Some kibbutzim (of the Mapai-oriented Federation, *Ichud Hakvutzot Vehakibbutzim*) have introduced what is called the "personal budget" into the restricted area of clothing. Instead of fixing norms, each member is provided with a fixed and equal sum of money with which to buy whatever clothes he thinks fit. They are of the opinion that this "liberalisation" is the solution to the problem of freedom of choice.

The Kibbutz Artzi is opposed to these tendencies and believes that collective consumption is indivisible. For if the kibbutz cannot decide collectively on clothing, why should it be more capable of deciding collectively on economic, social and educational matters? If freedom of choice is better served by the personal budget in clothing, why should it not be extended so as to give "a wider freedom of choice" in food and education, culture and recreation?

The personal clothes budget is fixed, so that within its limits a family must make ends meet without the advantages of buying in quantity and of manoeuvrability in satisfying individual needs which

* There are some twenty settlements of the "Moshav Shitufi" type, based upon the kibbutz principle of collective production and the moshav principle of individual consumption. Income is equally divided between families according to the number of children and dependents in each household.

the clothes-store enjoys if it caters for all and approaches different requests flexibly and equitably. If, under the personal budget, a member buys badly, loses a garment or has it spoiled, or if the calculation goes wrong, as it can so easily do for innumerable reasons, the member is not able, like a person outside, to put things right by cutting down on another budget. Neither can the clothes-store be approached for help. Only two alternative correctives exist: either the budget must be raised, in which case it must be raised for all and this is impractical; or it must be extended to include other areas, so as to give the same maneouvrability enjoyed by a city family or the kibbutz clothes-store. This is the real danger— that the personal budget is the thin end of the wedge and that in the long run it cannot be limited to one field.

There are other disadvantages as well. If the personal budget includes working-clothes, for example, this is a possible cause of inequality, for the wear and tear on a teacher's clothes is far less than on that of a worker in the fields. A member receiving gifts of clothing is at an advantage, whereas under the norm-system gifts can be taken into account. And if through saving soap, more chocolates can be bought for the children, commodities become valuable not in themselves but according to their worth in terms of money, which takes us back to the capitalist method of evaluation.

It is claimed that collective consumption is wasteful, for there is more respect for "private" than for collective property. There may be a grain of truth in this, and it is a real problem. But the limited personal budget in clothes does nothing to solve it, for nobody would suggest that a tractor or a milking-machine could be privately owned in the kibbutz. Such a problem must be tackled at the roots and not by piecemeal compromises.

In fact, the whole concept of the personal budget is contrary to the two fundamental principles of collectivism and equality upon which the whole of the kibbutz system rests. While it sets out to satisfy freedom of choice—which can be achieved without it, even if this is not easy—in effect it heralds the introduction of alien concepts into the collective. Once one does away with the principle that the commune provides the members' needs, and that these are decided upon collectively by the commune as a whole, the way is wide open to the eventual adoption of a system based upon "to each according to his work" rather than his needs. This would of course spell the end of real equality in the kibbutz.

However, it cannot be stressed too strongly that a system more in keeping with kibbutz principles must also meet the legitimate and very understandable demand to leave wide scope for individual choice within a framework of equality and not of standardisation. Failing this, the "personal budget" will always beckon to the dissatisfied kibbutz members, especially women, as the simplest way out. In the K.A., the norms system is now operated in such a way as to give a large degree of choice year by year, enabling members to choose within a whole range of possibilities rather than receive clothes automatically. Though this system, too, depends to an extent on the people responsible for putting it into practice, it has met with general approval.

It seems to be popular and practical, helping to do away with the feeling that kibbutz forms provide insufficient room for personal choice. As such it is a good example of the never-ending search for changes which meet the needs of the new and more sophisticated times in which the kibbutz is developing without sacrificing the principles upon which the kibbutz system is founded.

WHERE ARE THE LIMITS?

Hundreds of threads bind the kibbutz to the world outside it through family relationships and friendships. What happens, then, when a member receives a gift from Israel or abroad? If it is something small—a book, a vase, a picture—this presents no problems, but with larger items, both those which the kibbutz provides and those which it does not, things are not easy. Everything depends upon whether or not it enables one family to enjoy a higher standard of living than another.

For example, thousands of members received reparation money from Germany. In the Kibbutz Artzi it was decided that this money must belong to the kibbutz, and it was used to build swimmingpools or cultural centres, or to provide other amenities, for such large sums were involved that they could have led to serious differentiation between members. (In some kibbutzim, a small sum of money was placed at the disposal of members who received reparations, to spend as they pleased.) This was a most serious test of principle, and because the kibbutzim did not evade the issue, and were not afraid to approach it openly and boldly, they emerged from it honourably, without forfeiting principles and to the satisfaction of the overwhelming majority of the membership.

But not everything in the garden is rosy, and kibbutzim which fail to set clear limits between what is permissible and what is incompatible with kibbutz equality find themselves in the grip of a vicious circle which it is hard to break. There were times when the kibbutz was so austere that the idea of providing an electric kettle for every room aroused long discussions. Things are very different now and standards incomparably higher. The kibbutz provides, and provides equally, not only basic needs but many other facilities which make life easier and pleasanter. Though many kibbutzim cannot yet provide a record-player or an electric razor, it is usually not considered that gifts like these undermine equality; but the collective must decide where to draw the line, and different kibbutzim have different tendencies and traditions in these matters. But as people receive more, they want more, and the problems of preserving basic equality grow rather than diminish.

What is more, the principle of equality is so engrained in the kibbutz that because it has been realised in over 90 per cent of all those factors which make up what we call standards of living—a unique achievement if ever there was one—people are more sensitive to those breaches and transgressions which do exist. This is why it is so important not only to ensure that the collective provides more and more everyday needs, but that public opinion be strong enough to nip undesirable tendencies in the bud before they become dangerous enough to poison the atmosphere. The smallest inequalities, which are quite insignificant in themselves and which outside observers would find it hard to distinguish, can cause dissatisfaction and jealousy in these small and closely knit communities.

Lack of privacy also presents a problem to some members, though, as we shall see, the kibbutz family is extraordinarily strong and secure. Though not all small talk is malicious, some are of the view that in its exaggerated tendency to gossip the kibbutz has taken over one of the less positive features of village life, and this is rather surprising in view of the high cultural standards and broad intellecutal horizons of most kibbutz members.

THE INDIVIDUAL AND THE INSTITUTION

In modern life, people are more and more dependent upon the institutions and machinery of governmental and other authorities. They have no alternative but to turn to the anonymous official in whom authority is vested. The kibbutz, too, has become more institutionalised, and there is "an address" for nearly every request or complaint. The difference is that this is not an anonymous bureaucrat occupying a small room in an enormous building, but a kibbutz member who is your equal, whom you know well, and whom you have elected for a short term of office. He may be your neighbour or workmate, have a child in your own child's group, have grown up with you in the youth movement abroad or in the children's house in the kibbutz.

Nevertheless, though you may know him and trust him, you are dependent upon him. It is a fallacy to think that this interdependence can be eliminated by more, or more detailed, regulations, by a sort of written constitution or contract covering every eventuality in kibbutz life.

The contrary would appear to be true: regulations are necessary and positive, but the more hidebound and dogmatic they become, the less room they leave for that understanding and flexibility which kibbutz members rightly expect from those in office. Members are sometimes unhappy about the way in which their request is treated by a committee or by the member responsible for a particular area. But more often than not, for example, if there is a desire to change one's place of work, it is not the rejection of the request which hurts, but the way in which it is rejected. The style of the discussion, rather than its content, leaves a bad taste.

This depends in equal measure upon both parties to the negotiation. A request can be posed as an ultimatum, which shows no understanding of the committee's problems in weighing up different requests objectively and fairly. On the other hand, the committee must prove that it is genuinely concerned to help, that it gives everyone a sympathetic hearing and explains its decision clearly and objectively. This is why a purely administrative approach can never succeed in the kibbutz. Those in office must perform their tasks, large or small, with exactly the same understanding with which they expect to be treated when they are out of office.

The kibbutz structure makes this possible. Though there are exceptions, this is the dominant trend, so that the social contract binding a member to elected institutions is founded on good faith, mutual understanding and comradeship. He does not feel like a tiny cog in a bureaucratic machine over which he has no control and which, in its very nature, is incapable of understanding the problems of the individual. This sense of freedom, of being master of one's own fate, of real possibilities to influence and to shape large decisions as well as small, stands in stark contrast to the increasing alienation of man in modern mass-society.

CHAPTER 7

New Society — New Man?

WE HAVE spoken of the relations of people to work, to democracy and to equality, and this must bring us to the question: if the kibbutz is the prototype of a better society, are we able to find developing within it a better man, corresponding in his spiritual make-up and outlook to the new form of human—and not only organisational—relations of the new society?

Georges Friedmann of the University of Paris, an international authority on the sociology of work and one of the most understanding observers of the kibbutz to record his impressions in recent years (see his oddly named *The End of the Jewish People?*, Hutchinson, London, 1967), has wisely remarked that "kibbutz people are neither angels nor supermen and deserve something better than blind admiration or stupid moralising". The kibbutz vision can only come to complete fruition when a new man will realise it. The collectives are, from this point of view, "before their time". But Friedmann also notes that "the reality of human relations, whether in Moscow or a kolhoz is more remote from the ethical ideal laid down in Marx's philosophy (e.g. in relation to the role of money, the conflict between manual and intellectual labour, and family life) than it is in an average Israeli kibbutz. The latter is more than a contribution to the micro-sociology of socialist societies; it is on a limited scale, an original and successful application of socialist principles."

TOWARDS A NEW PERSONALITY

The late Shmuel Golan, of Kibbutz Mishmar Haemek, one of the pioneers of the theory and practice of communal education, has left us a rich heritage of reflections upon this question. We say reflections, because the question is far too deep, and a few decades of kibbutz experience far too short, to permit of categorical answers. Nothing is more dangerous here than to fall into the trap of superficial extremism, be it positive or negative. Those who imagine that the heritage of the past has been eliminated overnight by the waving of a magic wand are as wrong as those who conclude that because there is light and shadow in kibbutz life and its members are not yet "perfect", human nature cannot be changed, so that the whole effort has no point. For both these extremes of optimism and pessimism can lead to the same type of fatalism, cynicism and loss of faith in man.

Shmuel Golan explains* that, in general, human relations reflect different conditions of life. They change as society changes. Anthropologists know of societies where the dominant theme is friendly co-operation and of those where aggression and jealousy are dominant. We know, too, that human consciousness lags behind the development of the relations of production, and that heredity is an important and an independent factor. Unlike economic changes, psychological changes take place slowly, over generations, so that during transition periods man's consciousness contains elements of new and revolutionary ideas side by side with the heritage of the past.

Enormous reserves of brotherhood, solidarity and readiness to sacrifice come to light in revolutionary periods. At such times, man can be gripped by a vision which takes precedence over all egoistic considerations. But when the crisis is over and instead of its inspiration, men face the prosaic aftermath, revolutionary fervour declines and fewer answer the call for pioneering and self-sacrifice.

For example, the very early days of the kibbutz showed like a laboratory experiment that the acquisitive or property instinct was subordinated to the deep satisfaction which came with an intensive social life and the joy of creation. But today the property instinct reappears; in a society which has achieved almost complete

* In a volume of his collected writings, *Sugiot Hakibbutz*, published in Hebrew by Sifriat Hapoalim.

equality, there may even be a glaring disproportion between the modesty of demand and the depth of emotion which it engenders, showing that the capitalist heritage is at work.

Capitalism is competitive, exploitative, individualistic and acquisitive. The kibbutz is its antithesis—equal, collective, democratic and free. But the reflection of the new society in the psychological makeup of its members is not yet stable, especially since the kibbutz is surrounded by, and is subject to, capitalist influences. The old and the new coexist, compete. The new characteristics start as conscious "additions" to man's behaviour. Constantly supported by public opinion, they grow and take root, stemming but not destroying the resurgence of opposing tendencies inherited from the past and strengthened by influences from outside. Current kibbutz experience endorses the hope and belief that over the course of generations the new characteristics will take deeper roots in, and become part of, man's personality.

BETWEEN THE OLD AND THE NEW

In this respect, the kibbutz is in the transition period from the old to the new. *If it is too early to speak of a "new man", it is undoubtedly true to speak of a society living according to new values. Though they still exist consciously and subconsciously, the values of the old society stand condemned. The obligatory norms of behaviour, those which the society respects and encourages, have changed basically, so that the ideal toward which man strives is now in keeping with the ideals of the new society.* Brotherhood and mutual aid, prostrated by competitive-acquisitive society (except in time of war and crisis), or largely restricted to the family, become the heritage of the whole society. In the organic kibbutz, human relations become closer, more direct and intimate, so that in this respect the kibbutz aims to resemble an extended family.

Within its framework, human conflicts do not vanish. Competition, though it is for social respect instead of material wealth, can still be conducted aggressively, leading to jealousy and even hatred. Friendships can be broken, confidences betrayed, pride wounded and ambitions thwarted. Some such conflicts leave permanent grudges, even if some are absorbed into the stream of life and leave no trace.

But nobody in the kibbutz is left to his fate while life around him carries on regardless, apathetic to individuals' problems and psychological conflicts. The problems of the individual concern society and society does everything possible to meet them. The individual knows that he is not deserted by society, even if this has an apparent disadvantage in a framework as intimate and "concentrated" as the kibbutz. In the city, all this is hidden from the public eye, and no such help can be expected, except from family and close friends. The struggle for existence in competitive society leaves little room for real concern about others' problems or for genuine mutual aid. Among people who must "look after their own interests", how often do we hear that "I'm all right Jack" and "it's each man for himself and the devil take the hindmost"?

All too often, individual "success" is only achieved through the ruthless destruction of would-be competitors. In the kibbutz, the ethics of the rat-race have been replaced by social relations which, if they have not yet abolished conflict, can face it openly and boldly, thus holding out real hope of its ultimate solution.

SOCIAL CHANGES AND HUMAN CHANGES

In these reflections we have tried—in our own words and on our own responsibility—to paraphrase no more than a tiny fragment of the rich heritage which Shmuel Golan bequeathed in his writings to students of kibbutz society. They do full justice neither to the man nor to the subject, for both are infinitely deeper and broader than can be expressed in a few pages.

There can be little doubt that kibbutzim differ quite considerably in their social atmosphere and mentality according to their particular composition—land of origin, conditions of life abroad, education, etc. (A new element is, of course, introduced into this social kaleidoscope by the increasing numbers of young men and women born and educated in the kibbutz.) Individuals certainly come to the kibbutz with various degrees of psychological balance as a result of their former background and experience. These differences presumably make it easier or harder for them to adjust their behaviour-patterns to those of the new society. Personal tragedies, ill-health and internal family relationships also influence people in the kibbutz, as elsewhere.

Summing up one of his articles, Shmuel Golan observes:

> If the factors undermining comradeship, solidarity and mutual aid are founded in the existing social order, then they are destined to subside and disappear (with) the foundation of a new society and regime. In a regime which will do away with the exploitation of man by man, will redeem mankind from starvation and unemployment, will put an end to tyranny and persecution—there will no longer be room for hatred, suspicion and lack of faith, in so far as their roots are social (and the social factor is the dominant factor). Naturally, this change will not take place overnight, or automatically: it will be slow and gradual from a psychological point of view.
>
> The kibbutz can serve as an example of these changes. *The fact that there is no longer any objective foundation for the traditional hostile relations leaves its imprint upon the relations between people in the kibbutz.* Aggressive manifestations are restrained, and the collective conscience becomes the primary force determining man's way of life. Life is conducted without the need for formal sanctions: work is done without a supervisor, morality does not need to be defended by priests, judges and policemen. Mutual aid is transformed into the highest law of life, and cooperation between comrades is the only guarantee. . . . In principle, kibbutz morality has won a great victory.
>
> Conscious effort and the activisation of public opinion to react to regressive symptoms in the relations between individuals are likely to transform the objective achievements into subjective attributes—to instill good comradeship in the consciousness of men and to advance the tempo of psychological changes so that they will correspond to social changes. . . . Individual manifestations of comradeship are to be found in all societies, and there is nothing new in them. What must distinguish kibbutz society is the conversion of comradeship into a general norm or standard, into conscious behaviour, into a style of life. We do not delude ourselves: disputes, clashes, jealousy, conflicting interests and inflamed instincts will never be abolished of themselves. But in the kibbutz, there is room to lay bare their roots, to uncover their real causes, to prevent personal injuries and insults, to nuture cooperation and comradeship, for these are rooted in the very essence of kibbutz society.★

★ From an article on "Social Relations and Social Regime" in *Sugiot Hakibbutz*, by Shmuel Golan, pp. 42–43.

CHAPTER 8

Collective Education

THE fundamental aim of the educational system in the Kibbutz Artzi, which is known as collective education (*Chinuch Meshutaf* in Hebrew), is to ensure the continuity of kibbutz values. Though over the years it has developed into a school of education in its own right, it is not a detached educational theory, but endeavours to translate into educational terms the basic values of kibbutz society— labour, equality, collectivism, democracy and voluntarism. Its educational and psychological precepts are inseparable from the theory and practice of kibbutz life, from the ideology of the kibbutz as a value in itself and as an instrument for the national and social liberation of the Jewish people.

Nevertheless, collective education has aroused considerable interest among educationalists abroad, many of whom, including some who are far from identifying themselves with the kibbutz, have found in its education much that appears to be of more than local importance. Because it is one of the most original and revolutionary innovations of the kibbutz movement, it has also been the object of many great misconceptions. In this chapter, we can do no more than explain its structure and discuss briefly a few of its major implications.*

* For much of the material in this chapter, we are indebted to the writings of the late Shmuel Golan, which have been collected in his book, *Hachinuch Hameshutaf*, published in Hebrew by Sifriat Hapoalim. See also *Collective Education in the Kibbutz* by Shmuel Golan and Zvi Lavi, a pamphlet published by the Education Department of the Kibbutz Artzi Hashomer Hatzair, Merchavia, Israel, 1961, from which we have quoted widely in this chapter.

THE CHILDREN'S HOUSE

The most controversial aspect of collective education is that from birth onward the children live in separate children's houses, where they are under the care of professionally-trained kibbutz members. Every day, when the parents have finished work, the children come home to stay with them until bedtime.

Experience has strengthened the conviction that the parents are the most important factor in the education and healthy development of their children. Collective education does not question the unique emotional ties between parent and child, so that the problem has not been how to weaken them, but on the contrary—how to make them into a more stable and permanent source of security, and how to integrate them into education for communal life.

The children's houses in the kibbutz are specially planned in order to cater for the overall needs of a particular age group, including bedrooms, a kitchenette and dining-hall, playroom and workshop, toilet and showers, sheltered courtyard equipped with sand-box, gymnastic equipment and a pool, and classrooms for children of school-age. Both the building and the facilities are, of course, adapted to the varying needs of different ages, but they are all inclusive units for living and learning. Table 1 shows the different stages through which the children pass as they grow up.

The Infants' House

For the first six weeks of the baby's life, the mother is released entirely from her work in the kibbutz and devotes herself exclusively to feeding and looking after her child. After this, she returns to work, starting with 4 hours and gradually working further hours until weaning. She breastfeeds and/or feeds her baby, changes him, dresses him, plays with him and puts him to bed. Apart from this, a trained nurse (*Metapelet*)⋆ looks after the baby, attends to him if he

⋆ The Hebrew word *Metapelet* is not adequately translated by the words "nurse" or "house-mother". It has a broader and more comprehensive sense of house-mother and educator.

TABLE 1

	Age	No. in group	Educ. workers	Study hours	Work hours
Infants' house	Birth to 1¼	—	Infants' nurse Metapelet	—	—
Toddlers' house	1¼–4	6	Metapelet	—	—
Kindergarten and transition-kindergarten (Grade 1)	4–7	18	Kindergarten teacher, 2 Metaplot	Flexible	Flexible
Childrens' community (Primary School Grades 2–6)	7–12	18	Teacher, Metapelet	4–6 hours per day	Up to 1 hour
High school	12–18	25	Teacher, Metapelet	34 hours per week	12–13: 1 hr. 14–15: 2 hrs. 16–18: 3 hrs.

is ill, and gives guidance to the mother, especially to the young and inexperienced mother.

The routine in the babies' house is flexible enough to ensure maximum consideration for the individual needs of the baby. If he is not quiet at night, the mother may sleep close to him, in a special room. A nightwatch remains on the premises all night, and older children are supervised by two members who make rounds of all the children's houses. (When necessary—in special cases—an adult sleeps with the younger children.) Mothers and fathers are free to come and go as they please in the babies' house with their other children, and the atmosphere there is friendly and informal.

Confident that her baby is getting the best possible care,★ the mother is free to devote herself to the tasks of motherhood (which in any case involve emotional strains) without the additional worries of looking after the rest of the family, laundry, cooking, etc. After a few months, the child comes home every afternoon, and the parents' room becomes a place of major importance in his life. Gradually, too, the emotional ties between the child and his *Metapelet* are strengthened as she increasingly provides most of his needs, as are those between the child and the group with which he lives. These three centres—the parents, the *Metapelet* and the group—are to be the decisive influences on the child, and as he grows up, a fourth—the kibbutz itself—completes the picture of his educational environment.

The Toddlers' House

A permanent *Metapelet*, who worked with the children as babies, now takes over entire responsibility for the six children of the group. The child learns proper eating habits, cleanliness and discipline, how to dress and play independently. From the age of three, individual and spontaneous play are gradually supplemented by a coordinated programme which takes in short walks, stories and songs, organised games, gymnastics and crafts, for all of which the house and its surroundings are well equipped.

At four or five o'clock in the afternoon, the children come home. For 2 or 3 hours they play with their parents indoors or on the lawn, have tea, chat, or stroll round the farm. Each room has a children's corner, where the child keeps his own toys and can draw or play. At bedtime, the parents go back with the children to the children's house, kiss them goodnight and the *Metapelet* gives them supper or a snack and puts them to bed with a song or a story. Many parents like to drop in at night to make sure their children are sleeping well or to tuck them in.

In the last year, two groups of six which have been living side

★ The infant mortality rate in the kibbutz is among the lowest in the world—16·8 per 1000, as against 26·9 for Israel's Jewish population.

by side are united, and later a third group joins to make up the complement of the kindergarten.

The Kindergarten

This is an age when the child's faculties, his senses and physical skills are given every possibility of wider and more systematic development. Though there is much free time—for free play, voluntary help around the house, visits to the parents at work, or exploring the farm, organised collective activities now become more important. These include gymnastics, calisthenics, musical education, verbal self-expression, clay-modelling, crafts and acting. Walking in the farm and surroundings of the kibbutz, the group begins to appreciate the wonders of nature and to see the changing agricultural seasons. These outings become the subject for story-telling, discussion and creative activity at the evening gathering. Many handicrafts are taught, and there is work in the garden and with animals, so that the children begin to strike roots in the land and to feel the rhythm of the agricultural year.

During the last year, at the age of 6–7, called "transition kindergarten" and replacing the first grade, the children are introduced to the basic techniques of reading, writing and arithmetic, which should be mastered by the age of 8. Teaching is individualised, but more emphasis is now placed upon discipline, the obligations of the child to the group, mutual aid and group-solidarity. During this period, the children remain closely attached to their parents' room and the family circle.

Elementary Education

The children's community, as it is called, consists of children from the second to the sixth grade, ages 7 to 12. The children do much of their own housework and run a special children's farm where they look after chickens and ducks, sheep and goats, pigeons, rabbits, a donkey, etc., and grow flowers and vegetables. In addition to 4 to 6 hours of study every day, they are involved in an intensive programme of social, cultural and sports activities: parties for birthdays and festivals, performances and exhibitions, outings and hikes, cinema and children's theatre. Group loyalty and solidarity is now highly developed, and the childrens' community may already elect its own committees with the help of the teacher. Thus the community and the group (class) begin to demand from the child a higher degree of social discipline, responsibility and mutual aid, under the supervision of an educator who is not only a teacher but a counsellor and confidant of each child.

The Secondary or High School

Some particularly large kibbutzim have a school of their own, but two or more settlements of Hashomer Hatzair usually operate a regional boarding-school, from which the children come home at weekends and once or twice during the week. There may be from 100 to 300 pupils, divided into classes rarely exceeding 25, in which children from different kibbutzim are mixed. Unlike the younger children's houses, the whole school stands in its own grounds at some distance from the kibbutz.*

The large teaching staff which is provided by the kibbutzim is trained at two- or three-year courses in seminaries operated jointly by the three main kibbutz movements. Though its external appearance and excellent equipment are similar to a good high school elsewhere, its uniqueness is expressed in its constituting an independent children's community or village, largely run by the children themselves, in which academic learning and agricultural work are totally integrated. It is a sort of democratic republic of youth, striving to establish its own pattern of life and mores. Youth is considered to be a value of its own in which there is no place for the superficial artificiality of "juke-box culture". Far from trying to copy the more negative symbols of grown-ups—smoking,

---

* Children from outside the kibbutz are also accepted in some cases and there are about 500 of them at present. Many of them opt to join the kibbutz after army service. About 4000 pupils learn in twenty-seven Kibbutz Artzi high schools.

make-up, over-sophistication in dress or promiscuity in relations between the sexes—the school must educate towards the type of working youth whose social and personal relations, outlook and basic values will enable him to become a conscious and responsible member of the kibbutz collective.

An intensive schedule of studies (6 hours), work (up to 3 hours), homework, social, cultural and sports activities fill up nearly every moment of the day. The students work both in a special training farm under the direction of expert instructors (and in the school dining-hall and household), and in the kibbutz farm, where in their last years they join the work-force of a particular branch. Here they will also work during a part of the vacation, so that during high school they gradually become fully integrated into the kibbutz farm.

With the help of the teachers, who play more of an advisory than an executive role at this age, the school community runs its own affairs through committees elected by the student body: for work, social affairs, editing the school bulletin, sport, culture, etc. Social and cultural life—in the framework of the group, the whole school, or the Hashomer Hatzair youth movement to which all the children belong—incorporate a range of activities far too wide to be detailed here, including trips, outings to place of interest (factories, theatres, concerts, exhibitions) and long hikes or camps which take the children all over the length and breadth of Israel.

Musical and artistic education are particularly highly developed, and each school has its own choir, dramatic circle and orchestra (there is also a combined symphony orchestra of pupils in the kibbutz movement, since those who show particular talent are also encouraged to learn instruments).

Handicrafts are on such a high standard that it is often hard to believe that some of the crafts exhibited at the end of the school year are not the work of professionals. Outside the regular curriculum, the children can choose between a number of evening study circles, such as literature, politics, dancing, art, agriculture, etc.

PARENTS AND CHILDREN

Having glanced at the structure of kibbutz education, we can now discuss a few of its special characteristics.

The old story about the tourist who was surprised to see that kibbutz children recognised their parents is no longer very funny. Indeed, all evidence shows that the relations between parent and child in the kibbutz are certainly no less loving than those in private households. It is naïve to suggest that there is a sort of absolute mathematical formula stating that the amount of love and the amount of time spent together are directly proportional. Quite apart from the fact that many mothers in town go out to work, we know how hard it can be for the harassed housewife not to become angry and impatient with the little child who hangs on to her apron strings while she is hurrying to finish her housework. And how often does father come home from work only in time to kiss his children goodnight and hear from their mother how the day passed.

In the kibbutz, the meeting between parents and children is far more harmonious. It takes place in a relaxed atmosphere after work, when for 2 or 3 hours both parents can devote themselves—to the exclusion of other worries—to their children. For all concerned, this is the happiest and most eagerly anticipated time of the day.

Though nearly all parents are capable of loving their children, they can unknowingly make the most harmful educational and psychological mistakes with them, and this even if their family life is free of those strains and tensions which can play havoc with a child's mental health.

Kibbutz education ensures that the parents can give their children that degree of love and attachment which will guarantee a sense of security, but it minimises the negative influence of such mistakes, whatever their cause: for example, the excessive love of an over-anxious mother, or total misunderstanding of the real reasons for what is called "disobedience", "defiance", "ungratefulness" and so on, which can make family life a nightmare of friction, clashes and recriminations.

It is undeniable that nobody can love their children like parents, but far more doubtful whether this automatically makes them all the most suitable people to accept exclusive responsibility for educating them. For example, the harsh demands made upon the young child by toilet training require much real understanding and a quiet, objective approach. An excess of love and laxity, or of exhortation and impatience, are equally bad counsellors. In the kibbutz, this type of sensitive educational and psychological problem is taken out of the subjective hands of the mother and entrusted to the more objective and trained hands of the *Metapelet*. This both minimises the potential mistakes of some parents and does away with the friction which this can cause in the family circle.

Some of the criticisms of communal education would be better founded if family life outside the kibbutz were always an idyll, if all parents were in the nature of things equally capable of bringing up their children to perfection. In reality, this is unfortunately very far from the truth. In fact, the kibbutz system would seem to serve the interests not only of the children, but of both "better" and "worse" parents. It promises *optimal conditions for all*. It grants parental love and understanding its rightful place as a vital factor in the healthy development of the child and in the enrichment of child–parent relationships. At the same time, it minimises the detrimental influence of parents who in another framework would provide less adequate conditions, make more mistakes and therefore unwittingly hinder both the child's development and family harmony.

In individualistic society, each family must get along and rear the children as best it can. Since each family is independent, it can shrug off the problems of less successful neighbours—and children—with the attitude that "it's just too bad". The social contract of the kibbutz dictates that it provides optimal conditions for all its children. This is not because it rates the importance of the family less, but rather the opposite. It must ensure *the best possible education to all*. It therefore simultaneously fosters the emotional attachment of the child both to the family and to the wider community, striving from earliest childhood to do away with conflicts between the needs of the individual and those of the group.

The role of the father in communal education is far more important than we often see it in town. The kibbutz mother and father are both busy at work during the day while the child is in the children's house. When he comes home, he enjoys the undivided attention of the mother and father in equal measure. The father is no longer a rather distant figure of authority ("I'll tell your father about this . . .") whose presence demands special consideration from the children. Neither is he the breadwinner, demanding suitable respect and admiration. He "belongs to" the child no less than the mother, an intimate friend and confident, participating equally in the tasks of parenthood. (In this sense, collective education may be said to have "returned the child to the father".) Kibbutz members take this new relationship for granted, but how many working fathers elsewhere can afford the luxury of being able to spend 2 or 3 hours every day in the family circle?

To sum up, though the role of parents and family in communal education has changed, this has not been at the expense of the love and affection between parents and children. There may even be reason to believe that the opposite is nearer to the real truth.

EDUCATION FOR ALL

All kibbutz children without exception receive a full high school education. Since free and compulsory education in Israel covers only elementary school, this is a great financial burden on a workers' community like the kibbutz, involving expensive building, a large staff and smaller classes than those in town. Even today, there is some truth in the old saying that the kibbutz looks after the cows, the children and the members in that order of priority. In so far as this is humanly possible, the kibbutz gives the lie to the cynical idea that all people are born equal but that some are more equal than others. For it is not only a highly child-oriented society, but its education is unreservedly non-selective. In accordance with this principle of non-selectivity, no grades are given, no formal examinations held and no pupils held back a class.* Though its academic standards are high, kibbutz education is not concerned to cram the pupil with the maximum amount of pure knowledge. Real education—in the sense of the development of intellect, of personality, of character and of social values—and instruction, the inculcation of pure knowledge, are inseparable in the kibbutz school.

In the old-type school, the pupil is an object of instruction which is broken up and fragmented into a number of individual subjects with little organic connection between them. This tends to foster a passive attitude towards learning, divorcing theory from practice, pure knowledge from a broad and clear world outlook or philosophy of life, intellectual from physical work, and pupil from teacher. Claiming to make "equal demands", in practice it encourages a careerist interest in good marks among some students, while leaving others to their fate.

The kibbutz school is based upon respect for the individual personality and potential of each child, and upon mutual trust between pupil and teacher, rather than blind and impersonal discipline. It strives above all to nurture the intellectual curiosity and potential of the student, so that he can think and work things out for himself. Accordingly, it leaves wide scope for self-study and self-expression under the guidance of the teacher, so that the tempo and demands can be varied according to the individual potential of the child.

THE PROJECT METHOD

In order to achieve these aims, the kibbutz school has evolved a project method of learning, concentrating as much study as possible

* It goes without saying that corporal punishment at school or at home is absolutely unknown in the kibbutz. Asked what was his strongest impression of a week's visit to relatives in town, a kibbutz child unhesitatingly replied that he saw a mother hit her child for spilling the soup. One of the children in my kibbutz who was in England with his parents and attended primary school was cuffed over the ears for disturbing the teacher. To the latter's surprise, the child calmly stood up and hit him back! These reactions of kibbutz children are not altogether untypical, for the use of force by an adult is completely strange to them.

around a given theme. In the elementary school, for example, one of the early projects centres around the subject of "Indians". The children will make Indian costumes and tools, build an Indian encampment in the woods and live in the wigwams for a day and night. They will hear stories about Indians and dramatise them, learn their songs and poems and fill special notebooks with drawings, compositions, stories and sums on the subject. The classroom will be decorated accordingly, and the project comes to its head with an exhibition and presentation for the parents.

A later theme, transportation, involves visits to a port or aerodrome, a bus or railway-station—and again the children read, write and do their arithmetic around the theme. Among typical elementary school subjects, which may last from two to six weeks, according to grade, we find: our flock of sheep, birds, ants, the forest, wheat and bread, our kibbutz, the First of May, Jewish children, our ancestors, Joseph and his brethren, Jewish festivals,* etc.

The project method is also used at high school, but the subjects

---

* Kibbutz education is secular, but deeply traditional. All the major Jewish festivals (except the Day of Atonement) have a national-historical and/or agricultural significance. The children's participation in their celebration expresses their own roots in the soil as they bring in the first-fruits of their own farm, plant a tree on Tu'beshvat, or build their own Succot. Chanukah, with its unforgettable ceremony of the kindling of the lights, and Pesach, which is one of the highlights of the whole kibbutz year, recall episodes of Jewish heroism in the long struggle for liberation. Purim is a magnificent fancy-dress carnival, Lag Be'omer a sports festival. The children look forward to the festivals eagerly, for each one has a special excitement of its own.

The Bible is taught very thoroughly, for it is a major source, not only of all the early history of the Jewish people, of the Hebrew language and of the geography of Israel, but it has unique literary, ethical, moral and social values. These, rather than its purely religious significance, give it its special place in kibbutz education. Though formal religion has no place in the kibbutz, the history, culture, traditions and ethical values of the Jewish past play a major part not only in the study-curriculum but in the whole life of the kibbutz child. He lives with history as he learns to know and love his homeland, which is steeped in history. The kibbutz, which is the most creative laboratory of the revival of Jewish and Hebrew culture in the new Israel, could hardly do otherwise than give its children a deep Jewish education, linking their future as Jews with the rich heritage of their people.

are no longer completely integrated. The curriculum is split up into the humanities (literature, history, sociology, economics, etc.) and the sciences (physics, chemistry, biology and agriculture). Hebrew, foreign languages (English, which is started at elementary school, and Arabic), mathematics, gymnastics, drawing, music and handicrafts are taught separately.

No more than two themes are taught simultaneously; each is allotted as much as 12 hours a week, and large, unbroken study-units facilitate concentration and continuity. Though the high school is not an agricultural school in the narrow sense, practical and theoretical agriculture occupy an important part in the curriculum. A limited degree of specialisation in the last two years enables pupils to choose between agriculture–biology, physics–chemistry, and literature–sociology.

EXPLOITING THE CHILD'S POTENTIAL

Though it is without grades and formal discipline, learning is not voluntary or dependent upon the goodwill of the pupil. It is a social obligation, imposed by the personal authority of, and respect for, the educator, and by the authority of the group and of public opinion in the whole school. Discussions, written questionnaires, lectures by the students, exhibitions and other didactic devices take the place of those grades and punishments which compel the child to study even if he hates it, and are sometimes the cause of his hating it. Experience has proved that cramming for examinations, with all its negative implications, can be replaced by more positive motivations, for the desire to learn, the intensivity of the studies and the initiative of the students are certainly no less in the kibbutz school than outside it.

On the assumption that different levels of achievement will always exist in the classroom, "genius" may not be deliberately cultivated, but ample compensation is to be found in the atmosphere of mutual aid, of serious study and of individual creativity which pervades the whole student body, enabling every child to develop his particular potential to the full.

GROUP AND EDUCATOR

The basic educational unit on which kibbutz education is founded is, of course, the group. More or less homogeneous in age, and always bisexual, it varies in size from the six children in the toddlers' house to twenty-five in the high school. At all ages, it provides security and comradeship, binding the children together by a deep sense of belonging and loyalty, encouraging individual initiative, yet fostering the give-and-take of collective life. As the children age and mature, and particularly at high school age, the group becomes an all-inclusive organic unit, incorporating both the class and the youth movement—the focal point where all the spheres of life and activity of the wider community intersect.

Every child knows his fellow-members intimately, is confident that he can rely upon them, expects their understanding and is prepared to receive their criticism. The group helps him in his personal problems, but at the same time can call him to order and demand that he accounts for his actions. In free and frank discussions, it moulds the character of its members, stimulating, activising and criticising. It is the collective conscience of the youngsters' community which, under the guidance of the educator, is strong enough to set ethical, social and intellectual standards and demand their fulfilment by each individual according to his own potential and possibilities.

The educator and the youth leader (counsellor) in the youth movement framework are not authoritarian figures demanding discipline and respect by reason of their office. Unless their own personal example and personality can win them respect, they will not win it at all. This gives them great possibilities, but makes great demands upon them, for the whole structure, encouraging friendly guidance, also precludes impersonal regimentation. It is through the group that the educator's guidance is channelised, but it will be ineffective unless he is an intimate confidant of each child, fathoming the depths of his personality as an individual and not only as a member of the group.

The child's confidence both in the group and in the educator are preconditions of the latter's educational intervention, supervision and ability to influence. Therefore kibbutz education is anti-authoritarian, but it is not free in the sense that it assumes spontaneous educational progress. Though this may sound paradoxical, it is at once free and democratic, yet directed and exacting, just as it is equal and collective, yet neither uniform nor standardised. In a word, the values and character of kibbutz society itself are fully expressed in its education.

SOME DILEMMAS OF COMMUNAL EDUCATION

With all the achievements, kibbutz educationalists are wary of idealisation and well aware that their system is not free of problems and dilemmas. For example, its structure is such that in the younger age-groups decisive importance is attached to the *Metapelet*—to her personality, her training, her instinct for education and the continuity of her work. This is a vocation demanding unlimited devotion to the group (some of which may be at the expense of the time which the *Metapelet* spends with her own children), and vast resources of patience and understanding. Though no effort is spared to choose the most suitable candidates for the work, the choice is not unlimited and it would be futile to expect that all be endowed with the same ability, the same feeling for children and intuitive understanding of their problems.

Though training is all-important, it would also be unrealistic to assume that all *Metaplot* enjoy the same potential for exploiting the training facilities available. Though the *Metaplot* almost invariably work with exemplary devotion and receive wide satisfaction from their work, their own personalities inevitably influence their ability to avoid educational pitfalls (such as conscious or unconscious favouritism, over-regimentation or a lack of warmth towards the children).

Then there are *Metaplot* whose success with the children is not matched by an equal ability to communicate with the parents. This can be influenced by personal likes and dislikes on both sides, or simply by the heavy pressure of work, which makes it hard, with all the goodwill in the world, to ensure that close touch with the individual parents and with the parents as a body which is so important in communal education. Whenever such failures of communication appear, they do double damage: on the one hand they lead to dissatisfaction on the part of the parents, and on the other hand they hinder that co-operation and mutual confidence which are essential if both sides are to play their correct role in the educational processes to which the child is subject.

Over-frequent changes of *Metaplot* also constitute a problem, for especially in early childhood the group's close attachment to their *Metaplot* makes every change into a difficult period for them and temporarily undermines their security. It should also be noted that though there is room for flexibility in fixing the exact numbers in every group and slight variations from the norms are sometimes to be found, the demographic development of a kibbutz may occasionally make it hard to ensure that the more or less correct numerical framework is achieved without too large an age-range.

Far more serious is the feeling of some parents that very young children are not adequately supervised during the dark hours of the night in the children's houses. There is reason to believe that where such doubts arise, they are more the result of the insecurity of the mother than of the child—a throwback from the old and accepted systems of family education in which most of the parents have been brought up. The desire to be close to the little child at night is not easy to overcome for some mothers, however strong is the objective evidence that communal sleeping is good for the children. Perhaps this is the reason why in many of the settlements of the Ichud Hakvutzot Vehakibbutzim the children now sleep at home. The Kibbutz Artzi has rejected this change and prefers to devote its energy to improving existing arrangements* and educating those few parents who have doubts to recognise the fact, which all the evidence supports, that the child's interests are best served by main-

---

* A loudspeaker system enables the night watch to hear every sound in all children's houses and a child can also use it to ask the watchman to come. There is also an emergency lighting system worked on batteries in case the electricity fails.

taining the unity and integrity of communal education as it has crystallised in the kibbutzim.

At high school, the problems are of a different nature. For example, it has been increasingly recognised that even if kibbutz life were "faultless" (which is far from true!), the ability of the child to face his future in the army and the kibbutz is not served by his being too cut off, or sheltered, from the reality outside. A hothouse atmosphere can restrict the horizons of the kibbutz child and does not adequately prepare him for life.

To meet this very real and important problem, the schedule now includes a comprehensive plan of visits to towns and villages where the students can see for themselves during a few days' stay how the other 95 per cent live. Thus they feel the reality of city slums, of new immigrant children, of the Arab village, of a religious settlement, or of the moshav and of other kibbutz movements. The regular meetings at camps and on hikes, in seminars and conferences, with city members within the Hashomer Hatzair youth movement also present an opportunity to get to know and make friends with children from different backgrounds.

Many of the more basic problems of the high school cannot, however, be met simply by altering the curriculum. Since the kibbutz itself is now a most important part of the educational environment (and both are orientated toward the shaping of a new type of personality), many of the problems of the school are similar to, and influenced by, those of the kibbutz itself. Manifestations of anti-social behaviour, selfishness, apathy, disregard for communal property and so on are not absent even in a children's community, where the whole system of education, and its motivations, are directed against them.

Particularly in the last years of high school, it is the example of the kibbutz, of the parents' room, of the work-branch, which is no less important than that of the educator and the classroom. As the children mature, school and kibbutz merge and the real question becomes: with what sort of values will the younger generation enter kibbutz life? This is the overriding criterion with which the achievements and imperfections of kibbutz education must be measured.

THE EDUCATIONAL DEPARTMENT

Though it has formulated a definite and detailed organisational pattern which is closely followed in all the kibbutzim, collective education remains a series of guiding principles rather than a static formula. Through study and experience, it constantly evolves new ways of meeting both general problems, in which it can learn much from others, and more specific questions related to its own unique structure. This is one of the main functions of the Education Department of the Kibbutz Artzi, which lays down the pattern and standards of education and is responsible for the training and guidance of those who must carry them out in practice.

Neither the individual educator, nor the education committee and workers in each kibbutz are left to their own devices in the implementation of these complex processes. Through separate sections dealing with each age-group, and staffed by experts, the Education Department advises both on general problems and those of individual children in cases where professional help or treatment is deemed necessary. The Department convenes nation-wide conferences and further-study courses, and publishes two regular publications on theoretical and practical problems. It is able, therefore, to place at the disposal of every educator the centralised and accumulated experience of the whole movement.

This continuous and expert advice strengthens the ability of local educators and committees to deal with their problems, minimises the errors they might otherwise make, and enriches their work through utilising the experience of others facing similar dilemmas in their daily work.

AS OTHERS SEE IT

Perhaps kibbutz education is too young and revolutionary to enable those who are directly involved in it to avoid undue enthusiasm and idealisation. Among outside experts, there is no lack of prophets of gloom who claim that the "separation" of children from their parents must inevitably result in feelings of deprivation, in neuroses and in an institutionalised child. As against this, it is interesting to quote some of the views of Bruno Bettelheim, Professor of Psychology and Education at the University of Chicago, who writes:*

> From all available evidence, the results of kibbutz education are un-equivocal: the stated main goals are achieved to a degree that has no parallel in Western education. True, this is not what most American ob-servers report; nearly all of them have selected and interpreted data to support our own notions of child-rearing and personality development. But on the basis of my examination of the whole body of data, I am convinced that kibbutz education has had a success of a kind that might well lead us to reconsider some of our own assumptions and values throughout the entire field of education.

And elsewhere:

> Kibbutz children are actually much closer to their parents in some ways than most American children. . . . From toddlers' school on, the children take daily hikes to visit their parents at work. . . . (They) are stopped by adults, talked to, joked with, praised, perhaps asked to lend a hand, and when met by their parents, hugged. Thus the child is made to feel a welcome and important part of his father's and mother's activities and those of the whole community—an experience which most American children would envy greatly.

As for the end-result of kibbutz education, we might turn to the final sentences of a 500-page volume on the subject by Melford E. Spiro, *Children of the Kibbutz*,† much of which has met with strong criticism by kibbutz educationalists. Writing of the *Sabra* (Israel-born generation) in the kibbutz, he states:

> (He is) an efficient, productive and functioning adult. He is an adult with a sense of values and a conscience that assures the implementation of those values. He is motivated to carry on the basic features of kibbutz culture—its collective ownership, distribution according to need, agri-cultural work, collective rearing of children, and its devotion to intellec-tual and aesthetic values. In short, though his interpersonal relationships

---

* See the magazine *Commentary*, February 1962: "Does Communal Educa-tion work? The case of the Kibbutz."

† Published by Harvard University Press, Cambridge, Mass., U.S.A., 1958. The author is a professor of anthropology.

are somewhat disturbed, and his self-perception contains painful elements, the *Sabra* is not an 'institutional child.' He is—once the barriers of introversion and hostility are penetrated—a warm, sensitive, and, in some instances, gracious human being. . . .

YOUTH ALIYA

Youth Aliya* children have constituted an integral part of the human landscape of the kibbutz for over twenty-five years. Organised in groups of 30–40, they come from lands as different as Poland and Yemen, from the advanced countries of Europe and from backward, semi-feudal Asian and North African lands. Along with Israel-born boys and girls, the kibbutz accepts them with open arms, provides them with a home, and offers them an educational environment incorporating all that is best in the life of their new homeland.

It would be important enough if the kibbutz were merely to undertake the education up to the age of 18 of immigrant children who would otherwise be denied this and thrown on to the labour market to fend for themselves, untrained and uncared for. But as an egalitarian society which knows no social, class or ethnic distinctions, the kibbutz is a living example of the Zionist endeavour to merge all the ethnic groups which make up Israel's population into one working people, united by a common culture.

Dividing their day between study, work and an intensive social and cultural group-life, the children are gradually drawn into the atmosphere of kibbutz life, merge into its landscape and imbibe its values. Over the months and years, they undergo a transforma-

* Youth Aliya is that section of the World Zionist Organisation which is responsible for the immigration and absorption of Jewish children from abroad. Initiated in the early 1930's in order to save German-Jewish children from the Nazis, it first cared mainly for orphans and children from lands of persecution who were compelled to come to Palestine without their parents. In the State of Israel, many new immigrant families entrust their children to Youth Aliya for their education as a result of inadequate conditions at home, large families, or social problems. The organisation accepts children from the age of 13–14.

tion which makes it hard to recognise that the deep-rooted, sturdy, independent working-youths of 17 or 18 were once strange to each other, to the land, to the Hebrew language, to modern ways and co-operative life.

The educational premises are the same as the kibbutz high school, but the group generally maintains its own educational framework, suited to the special problems of instruction and education stemming from the different background of the children. As the parents are not in the kibbutz, the children are "adopted" by kibbutz families, where they are at once accepted into the family circle. Since in their later years they work half a day in the kibbutz farm and services, it is in the branch that the closest ties develop between the kibbutz and the youth group. At work, many of these children are no less than outstanding, quickly accepting responsibility, skilled, devoted and enterprising.

BRIDGING THE GULF

Yet if the education of kibbutz children has its problems they may look paltry compared to those facing the Youth Aliya educator. He must foster the values of a highly modern and progressive communal society among children whose harsh childhood has left many of them suspicious, distrustful, jealous and selfish. Strong barriers of hostility to new ideas of mutual trust and equality must be broken down if these children are to be won over and their misgivings to give way to a feeling of identification, of equality and of belonging. However harsh and exacting is this educational battle, the kibbutz accepts it because it offers a foothold in the "second" Israel, that of the new immigrants whose comparative poverty denies their children anything more than elementary education.

The Youth Aliya is a bridge between the old and the new, and no narrow considerations of profit or loss dictate its need or its dimensions. In 1966, there were about thirty groups in the Kibbutz Artzi, and 1000 youth. About ten new groups are absorbed annually.

Many of the youths (some 14 per cent of the kibbutz population are Youth Aliya graduates) come back to the kibbutz after the army and make it their home, a constant proof that the gulf between the old and the new can be bridged in a society where discrimination is unknown and equality of opportunity complete. Here they become teachers and youth-leaders in Hashomer Hatzair, branch-organisers and task-holders, marrying and bringing up their children to enjoy with them the privileges and obligations of kibbutz membership.

If it is inevitable that many—perhaps even the majority—of them will eventually build their lives outside the kibbutz under the pressure of parents and past, they do so as skilled workers for whom the dignity of labour has real meaning, as conscious and educated citizens with a sense of civic pride and patriotism, as people who have tasted of the fruits of culture and learned how it can enrich their lives. Wherever they decide to settle, the kibbutz has made them into better people, better citizens, better workers, and better parents.

In general, the kibbutz movement has attracted few members from the Oriental communities, who account for only 6·5 per cent of the total. This can be explained by the gulf separating immigrants from the more backward countries from the kibbutz in terms of social background and ability to adapt to new patterns of life. However, it is a failure all the more regrettable in light of a recent research project which showed that among the children of such immigrants in the kibbutzim, the educational achievements are indistinguishable from those of the general membership. Differences of background become unimportant in an egalitarian society.

The highest rate of marriage between Israelis of Eastern and of European–American origin is recorded in the kibbutzim, higher than in the cities or moshavim. One of the major tasks facing the kibbutzim in the coming years is to find ways and means of bridging the gulf separating the kibbutz from the oriental communities and their Israel-born children. Indeed, many observers rightly see this as a test which might determine the ability of the kibbutz to become a broad popular movement, as against the danger that its scope and influence be restricted or frozen in the period ahead. The future of the kibbutz depends on its impact upon the whole of Israeli society. It has shown that more than any other factor it can solve the problems of community integration but this must now be followed by a campaign of expansion aimed to bring more young people from the eastern communities to membership in the kibbutzim.

CHAPTER 9

The Hashomer Hatzair Youth Movement

FOR most of the members of the Kibbutz Artzi, education to the kibbutz did not start in the commune itself. The primary source lies in the educational youth movement of Hashomer Hatzair in Israel or abroad. The movement, which today encompasses Jewish youth in about twenty-five countries, has just celebrated its fiftieth anniversary. Founded in Eastern Europe on the eve of the First World War, it rapidly crystallised into the largest Zionist youth movement in the world, numbering no less than 70,000 members in 1939 when the Nazi holocaust which descended upon European Jewry destroyed its most deeply rooted centres. The postwar movement reflects the demographic changes in the life of the Jewish people after the catastrophe, and its main centres are in Israel itself and in the three surviving sectors of Jewish life: the Spanish-speaking (South America), the English-speaking (North America, England, South Africa and Australia), and the French-speaking (France and North Africa).

THE EDUCATIONAL TRADITION

The educational tradition of Hashomer Hatzair incorporates a number of different elements. Like the classical "free youth movement" which originated in Germany, it sees youth as having an independent value of its own, so that it is not a club organised by adults for youth but a movement of youth for youth. From the tradition of the boy scouts it took the ideal of youth at home in nature and outdoor life, able to use its hands as well as its mind, in a spirit of service and mutual aid.

120

Yet both these trends were unable to prevent the frittering away of the energy and idealism of their members for though they opposed urban conventions and the aping of worthless adult values, they offered for youth in their twenties no real alternative but to "adapt" to adult life. This was the great achievement of Hashomer Hatzair: the potential of idealistic youth was harnessed to a clearly defined goal—the construction of the commune in Israel, inspired by a crystallised Socialist–Zionist ideology. The revolt of youth was channelised into direct action.

As a result, the values of the youth movement—group solidarity, sexual equality, mutual aid, the feeling of oneness with nature, free and frank relations between young people, a happy and youthful yet at the same time earnest and serious approach to life, the rejection of double standards, the revolt against empty conformism, premature sophistication and social cynicism—all these become more than Peter Pan dreams cherished during a long weekend of camping only to be put aside in face of the need to grow up in a society which had no time for youthful illusions of brotherhood and "immature" idealism.

PERSONAL REALISATION

The very values scorned by the older generation became vital ingredients of the new type of personality required by the commune. And so the revolt of youth against adult hypocrisy became a part of a much larger revolt—against the indignity and insecurity of Jewish life in the Dispersion and against the whole false value-system of capitalism. Not satisfied with preaching armchair Zionism and lauding the working class and Socialism from afar, every senior member of Hashomer Hatzair has to live according to his convictions and face the ultimate implications of his revolt as a Jew and as a human being through *revolutionising his own life*. Personal realisation of his ideals in the kibbutz provides living proof that the values of the youth movement can be perpetuated in daily life. It enables the personal example of one generation to be handed down to another, and at the same time the kibbutz is not only a distant source of inspiration but sends back to the youth movement emissaries who embody the overriding principle of personal realisation in their own lives.

NATIONAL AND SOCIAL EDUCATION

Catering for Jewish youth from the age of 10 and into the twenties in the framework of closely knit groups of youngsters of a similar age, Hashomer Hatzair branches all over the world are founded upon unified educational and organisational principles. Though the conditions of Jewish life vary from place to place, the kibbutz and Israel orientation provides a common denominator. Broadly speaking, the programme—adapted, of course, to the needs of each age-group—incorporates three integrated educational motives: Jewish national education, Socialist education and character education.

Jewish education is of paramount importance as a barrier to the waves of assimilation to which Jewish youth is subjected in the Dispersion, and from the moment when the new member enters the movement centre, decorated with Hebrew slogans and pictures of Israel, he is brought into contact with the new secular culture of modern Israel. Modern Hebrew, Hebrew folk-songs and dances, Israeli symbolism, the celebration of Jewish festivals as in the kibbutz, and discussions and projects on the Jewish past, Jewish heroes ancient and modern, Zionist history and story of Israel today—all these help to kindle a sense of pride in, and identification with, the traditions of Jewish culture through the ages.

Socialist education stresses the dignity of labour, social justice and the brotherhood of nations and, in the older age-groups, involves more basic study of Socialist theory and practice. Whenever possible, the groups leave the city for the countryside, and scouting, hiking, handicrafts and camping help to develop a well-rounded and independent personality: an active and inquiring mind in a healthy body. Hashomer Hatzair youth shuns the symbols of urban sophistication such as flamboyant dressing-up, smoking, drinking and make-up, and strives to foster a youth culture of its own in which people are judged for what they are, dressing simply and aesthetically and enjoying life naturally and unaffectedly. In the centre of every educational project is the kibbutz itself, the personality and way of life of pioneers unreservedly devoted to their people and homeland.

By the early twenties, after years in which the values of Hashomer Hatzair increasingly became a part of the consciousness of the member as he accepts more and more responsibility for running the movement, he is ready to face the decisive test—the question of settlement in a kibbutz in Israel. This is the great Rubicon which every member must decide freely and consciously to cross. Those who decide against it can no longer remain in the movement, for personal realisation and example are its life-blood.

THE TRAINING FARM

In order to prepare movement graduates for kibbutz life, Hashomer Hatzair runs training-farms organised on kibbutz lines, which serve as a stepping-stone to a life of labour in the commune. Here the future kibbutz member receives his first taste of physical labour, of agriculture and of communal living. The group itself, with the help of an emissary from the Kibbutz Artzi, is responsible for the working of the farm and for the running of its own affairs: social, cultural and financial. The training-farm serves a number of related functions. It teaches work and agriculture, the patterns of communal living, sharing and equality, the Hebrew language; it enables pioneer groups who will settle together in Israel to get to know each other, to crystallise their group unity and loyalty, and to help each other overcome the revolutionary transition to a life of labour on the land—one of the most radical tests which any town-dweller has to face.

At the same time, the training-farm is a centre and source of inspiration to the youth movement in the city—a kibbutz within travelling distance of New York or Buenos Aires—a communal farm alive with the spirit of pioneering Israel, run by youngsters who only a few months before were youth-leaders in the town and spokesmen for the movement in the counsels of the Jewish community in which the movement works.

AGAINST THE STREAM

Like all vanguard movements, Hashomer Hatzair is a highly selective organisation, yet its strength has always lain in its deep attachment to the Jewish masses. In the dark and tragic days of the Nazi holocaust in Europe, it was no coincidence that the movement played a leading role in raising the banner of armed Jewish resistance to the German murder-machine. The young commander of the epic rising in the doomed Warsaw Ghetto was the head of Hashomer Hatzair in Warsaw—Mordechai Anielevich, whose death in the burning ruins of the ghetto transformed him into a symbol of modern Jewish heroism. Other members of the movement, some of whom lived to tell their stories to an unbelieving world, and are today kibbutz members, fought and organised resistance in other ghetto struggles and as partisans behind the German lines. Indeed, in every phase of the Jewish renaissance in Israel and abroad, graduates of Hashomer Hatzair played a prominent role wherever special courage and devotion were the order of the day.

Hashomer Hatzair has always founded its approach to youth on the conviction that youth is capable of great things when inspired by great causes. Its uncompromising demand for personal realisation in the kibbutz has often prompted the faint-hearted to question whether young people are capable of making such fateful decisions for themselves. But it is precisely this radicalism which has enabled the movement to perpetuate its values from generation to generation. To swim against the strong currents of careerism and cynicism which are so prevalent in the affluent urban Jewish life of the 1960's demands a degree of revolutionary fervour which is unlikely to be inspired by compromises and half-measures.

When, as in some of the South American countries today, the Jewish masses feel their insecurity and sense that they are living on the edge of a volcano, the position of the movement is stronger.

When, on the other hand, material affluence and the dead hand of conformism lull the Jewish community into a false sense of well-being, Hashomer Hatzair can do no more than maintain outposts in an environment often suspicious of its radicalism and indifferent to its idealism.

A radical youth movement is tested equally in both situations. Jewish history knows too many tragic examples of communities which woke up too late to an understanding that what was a lonely voice in the wilderness became overnight the voice of logic. For those who answered its call, and for those who may answer it tomorrow, the seventy-three kibbutzim of Hashomer Hatzair in Israel are the finest monument to the traditions of a movement which has always known that, in the words of a Jewish sage, "those who sow in tears shall reap in joy".

CHAPTER 10

The Family and the Woman in the Kibbutz

THE stability of the kibbutz family has been proved beyond any possible shadow of doubt, in spite of the conclusion of one sociologist who wrote that, strictly speaking, it does not exist at all! He was, of course, referring to the fact that the relationship of the family to the society of which it is a part has changed completely. It has no economic function, for collective production and consumption have replaced the family as the basic economic unit. Since men and women in the kibbutz are equal, the patriarchal foundation of the family has been destroyed. Though the family raises children, the family's function is no longer exclusively dominant among the factors shaping collective education.

SOURCES OF STABILITY

Far from undermining it, these changes have probably strengthened the stability of the kibbutz family and provide the foundations for a different, but richer family life. The economic factor plays no role in the formation of the kibbutz family, in its maintenance or—in the event of its failure—in its dissolution. By doing away with the economic, legal and spiritual dependence of the woman upon the man and on the economic function (which elsewhere can even dictate the maintenance of the family structure when man and wife feel they are no longer compatible), the kibbutz family rests upon positive personal, rather than impersonal economic, foundations.

Positive love, the desire to rear children together, the bonds of life companionship, sexual, emotional and spiritual partnership— these are the sources of the kibbutz family and its only mainstays. Of course, this cannot be expected to guarantee that the kibbutz family is always compatible and its internal life universally harmonious. The elimination of the economic factor makes it possible for people to choose their life-partners more objectively. A "good match" no longer depends upon good qualifications and jobs, good class or background, dowries and property. It depends upon people and not things: people as they are, without all the external paraphernalia which do much to determine who is suitable for whom in capitalist society.

Even without these elements of economic pressures, conventions and prejudices, on the basis of a free choice in which the only criterion is genuine compatibility, people can make mistakes, and particularly nowadays when the trend in the kibbutz is also to younger marriages, often in the early twenties (Divorce rates in the kibbutz are about the same as outside.) If proof were needed of the place of the family in communal education, we know that in spite of other factors (the *Metapelet* and children's house or community) a broken family may have the gravest repercussions on the children.

In general, the family in the kibbutz is certainly no less important than outside. Perhaps because of the restrictions of village life, even in this unique type of village, the family is more central and more basic to the happiness of kibbutz members than in the city. Communal services make the family room no less important, and the family circle (now embracing three generations in veteran settlements) remains the centre of communal, just as it is of individualistic, society. What is different is the basis which the kibbutz provides for the type of family, motivated exclusively by genuine love, comradeship, partnership, common interests and aspirations around which the life of the commune is built and with which it thrives and prospers.

We shall return to the theme of the younger generation in the kibbutz but it might be appropriate at this stage to mention another category of kibbutz membership—the old people. As their numbers increase, it is clear that quite apart from the relations between the generations, the extent to which old people will feel satisfied in the kibbutz is a vital problem in itself. After devoting a lifetime to his kibbutz, a man or woman will hope that in his later years he will not only be looked after but also surrounded by the sort of under-standing—some might call it "honour"—to which he is due. Indeed, one kibbutz leader has said that this will be a test for the quality of kibbutz life, for woe to a society which cannot provide maximum conditions for a contented old age. A special Department of the kibbutz movement is now dealing with the matter in its various aspects and it is hard to exaggerate the importance of this question.

EMANCIPATION AND EQUALITY

The emancipation of the woman and complete equality of the sexes was one of the most important goals of the kibbutz from its inception. It was among the most burning expressions of the revolt against bourgeois society, which inspired the founders of the kibbutz in the youth movement abroad, and from the earliest gropings towards the new communal society in the homeland.

The determination to free the woman from her traditional role as dependent upon the master of the house or breadwinner, and from exclusive subjugation to the household and to the children, was one of the sources of communal education. The communal nursery would open the road to real and not only formal equality. The woman would be free to do equal work and become an equal member of society, sharing equally in its obligations and privileges. This was both an economic need and an integral part of the kibbutz vision.

This vision has come to life in the kibbutz. As a wife, the woman is no longer economically dependent upon her husband, and as a mother no longer tied down remorselessly to her children. She is an equal member of the community, enjoying the complete security it offers her and her family, and the community has removed all those barriers which might prevent her from playing her equal role in every field of its life. Yet the realisation of this dream has probably been accompanied by deeper problems and a deeper consciousness of the disparity between the hope and the reality than in any other aspect of kibbutz life. Though, as elsewhere in kibbutz life, light and shadow exist side by side, it would be dishonest to deny that some of the problems of the woman in the kibbutz still await their complete solution.

Students of the kibbutz, along with rank and file members, both men and women, would probably not be able to give a unanimous reply to the question: what is the extent of this disparity, what are its roots, and in which direction is its solution to be found? Unless this problem is viewed dialectically, it is incomprehensible, for every new achievement as regards the woman in the kibbutz raises new responses, reactions and problems. Far from remaining static or in a vacuum, it is among the most dynamic questions in kibbutz life.

ACHIEVEMENTS AND DOUBTS

The woman is equal—but is she quite sure that she wants to be? May she not hanker after the old status, which has shaped her personality for countless generations, restricting her to deriving whatever satisfaction she may from her more restricted feminine world while her husband exploits the broad horizons which rightly belong to both sexes? The male is no longer superior in the kibbutz: yet is it not possible that as this objective process is consolidated, some men will react against it and try to express their feeling of superiority by showing off their male prowess within the family confines or even in public? True, public opinion will condemn both the pettiness of the woman and the prejudice and conceit of the man, but the legacy of the past dies slowly and may persist long after its objective basis—the male as father of the house and master of creation.

Many women have risen to the heights of achievement in kibbutz life and as representatives of the kibbutz in public life. They occupy the most important tasks in the kibbutz in all spheres, and have reached prominence as authors, poets and directors, painters and sculptors, dancers and musicians, politicians and public figures within the movement and outside it. Others have gained fulfilment and satisfaction in humbler tasks, through their own daily contribution to building the kibbutz and through raising a family to perpetuate its values.

Yet there may be a degree of truth in the sneaking feeling that a less talented man will sometimes be preferred to a more talented woman when the kibbutz elects its institutions year by year, and that those women who have reached such wonderful pinnacles of achievement may have had to fight harder to prove themselves, precisely because of their sex. In other societies, the woman may be torn between motherhood and career. Communal education does away with this contradiction between the conscience of a mother and wife and the woman's desire to express herself in other fields of activity.

The demands of motherhood impose some limitations but not enough to explain the following figures about task-holders in the years 1961–6, taken from a major survey of women in twelve representative kibbutzim of the K.A. among 466 women and eighty-five men in 1966 (see Table 1).

TABLE 1

	Women (percentage)	Men (percentage)
No task	55·4	40
Membership in a committee	24·6	18
Chairman of a committee or branch-organiser	16·3	34
Central task (Secretary, Treasurer, outside movement work)	3·7	8

In a different area, it is noteworthy that twice as many women as men stated that they are not prepared to speak in the members' meeting, even though there is little difference between men and women in attendance. It should not be overlooked that even after most of the work involved in maintaining the household has been socialised, and with most women working a 7-hour day, there remains a good deal which they may do outside working hours— looking after the room, cleaning, hand-washing, knitting, baking, etc. Most kibbutz members seem to take this for granted.

All this hints at the conclusion that kibbutz life may be harder for the women than for the men. Objective equality does not automatically overcome the heritage of the past, which is perpetuated in the psychology and make-up of men and women alike. What is in question is no longer formal equality and civic emancipation, but the exploitation of the unique opportunities offered by the commune to achieve that full equality which is inherent in its structure, yet whose full expression is held back by deep-rooted prejudices and negative influences from outside.

THE WOMAN AT WORK

The dominant question still awaiting an adequate solution is undoubtedly that of the work of the woman in the kibbutz. In the very early days of the kibbutz movement, it was naïvely assumed that equality would follow from the conquest by the woman of the hardest physical work. The illusions of this "romantic" period— with all its inspiration and all its errors—gave way to the more mature realisation that physical and biological differences exist and that equality cannot be measured in terms of physical prowess or muscular strength. The natural inclination of women for work with children and in the services became clear, and the objective scope and importance of non-productive work grew with the kibbutz.

A survey conducted in 1966 shows the following allocation of work among the whole female population of the K.A. (see Table 2). This shows that the wheel has turned full circle towards a concentration in education and the services and a relatively low proportion in agriculture and industry (especially in fifteen young and small kibbutzim with many children, where less shan 1 per cent of the women work in agriculture instead of the overall figure of nearly 9 per cent).

TABLE 2

	per cent
Education	36·1
Clothing (clothes-store, sewing, laundry)	18·5
Kitchen and dining-hall	13·2
Agriculture	8·9
Administration (includes accountancy)	4·3
Health	4
Industry	3·9
Full-time public activity	1
Outside work	0·6
Miscellaneous (crafts, illness, feeding mothers, etc.)	9·3

The overwhelming majority of women working with children and in education find in this vocation a source of satisfaction and pride, in spite of the long hours and hard work. Unfortunately, some of the kitchen work, for example, is for many not a vocation but a monotonous routine, taxing nerves and physical energy and giving inadequate satisfaction in return. Steps have already been taken in some settlements to shorten the working-day of the women (apart from the fact that older people in the kibbutz work less, according to a sliding scale). In 1966 the K.A. decided that wherever possible, mothers of two small children and all women over the age of 35 should work a 7-hour day.

It is true that work in a dining-hall or clothes-store catering for hundreds is a very different proposition from cooking or sewing within the narrow limits of a family. But the communal dining-hall must adhere to a rigid schedule and its workers come into contact with many people of different tastes, both of which raise the tension of work, leaving little time for relaxing the tempo. In general, what characterises the service branches is that work is done with people rather than with things, with a resultant strain on those responsible.

Perhaps even more important is the fact that, apart from education and to some extent work with young children, women receive less basic training than men for their work. The vast and continuing improvement in the physical conditions of work are not in themselves enough to ease the position of women in the services. Two other conditions would seem to be imperative: that the women be given a larger choice of jobs and that they receive more and better training, theoretical and practical.

The kibbutz in any case involves a limitation of the choice of jobs in comparison with the city but the women's feeling of equality is hampered by the seemingly unfavourable comparison with kibbutz men rather than with the city. In the survey mentioned, 60 per cent of the women thought that insufficient money was invested in service branches in order to raise their level. More and more is now being done to ensure that work in the services become a vocation characterised by high standards of equipment, organisation, expert knowledge of the work-process and professional know-how, all of which are so highly developed in agriculture and industry. The quicker this process moves forward, the larger will be the satisfaction of the woman at work.

Yet even in the kibbutz, rightly or wrongly there remains a difference between productive work and that which does not bring in direct income. The suitability of women for education does not preclude a conscious effort to ensure them a larger place in agriculture and industry. On the other hand, there is no natural law dictating that women are more suited to kitchen work (especially the less skilled and more unpopular work there which can be done in rotation for limited periods) and as the kibbutz develops there is both need and room to give the women a wider choice of jobs.

In the 1966 survey already mentioned, 28 per cent of the women said they would like to change their job (34 per cent said they did not originally want to work in their present places). Though we must be careful not to draw too far-reaching conclusions from very general questions, it seems safe to say that most kibbutz women identify themselves with the kibbutz way of life but retain reservations in some areas. After all, 70 per cent said that if one of their friends wanted to leave the kibbutz, they would do everything to persuade her to stay. If the kibbutzim will systematically tackle these pockets of discontent, which exist in various fields—consumption, education and probably above all satisfaction at work—this general feeling of identification can be deepened and fortified.

TASTE AND FEMININITY

The women want to be equal, but not the same, not only in the choice of clothes or furniture, which we have already discussed. They want to preserve their femininity, and the kibbutz needs their emotional warmth, their discretion in taste, their ability to make a room into a home, their feeling for beauty and refinement. "A thing of beauty is a joy for ever", and it is these innate womanly characteristics which ensure that kibbutz living will be warm and graceful rather than cold and institutionalised. If this was impossible in the harsh pioneering days (and even in the very young kibbutz today), the established kibbutz needs it in order to balance and enrich the lives of people so far removed from the crudity and boorishness of peasant life in a backward village.

Observers are often surprised to see how well dressed is the kibbutz woman after work, as if there were some innate contradiction between a woman's desire to preserve her appearance and the dictates of communal life. In fact, the contrary is true: good taste (as a value and not a snob-value) and the dignity of labour go hand in hand in a working society as cultured and progressive as the kibbutz.

We have noted the growing importance of the family circle in the consciousness of the kibbutz population in all age-groups, and not least among those born and bred in the kibbutz. In the 1966 survey it was shown that 58 per cent of the women interviewed (and 75 per cent of the grown-up daughters of the kibbutz) thought that the ideal family should have four or more children.

Because of the trend towards early marriage and the importance of the family, it has been decided to try and give kibbutz girls an additional year of study after their return from the army. These studies must not necessarily be connected with a particular job in the kibbutz as it is considered important to develop the broader cultural and intellectual inclinations of the young kibbutz woman, if possible before she is entirely taken up with her family responsibilities.

It must never be forgotten that the kibbutz is *a working society, which has abolished class distinctions.* Outside it, and in spite of formal equality, working-class women play an insignificant role in communal affairs, whereas the kibbutz woman has not only equal rights but also equal possibilities to exert her influence in shaping public opinion and influencing the society in which she lives through the democractic framework of committees and the general assembly.

Women in the kibbutz have therefore achieved a degree of equality which cannot be compared to that in other societies, and a unique degree of independence. Equality is guaranteed—but its potential is yet to be exploited to the full. The socialisation of household chores which enslaved the woman, the remarkable achievements of communal education and the new, equal contribution of the woman at work and as an equal partner in the kibbutz family—these are among the factors which provide objective conditions for the liberation of the woman from the taboos and restrictions of the past. In terms of possibilities and potential, the future of the kibbutz woman as an equal in the building of a new society is unlimited.

EQUALITY—FOR WHAT?

In effecting such a radical and revolutionary change in the status of the woman, the kibbutz has leaped forward into the future, raising hopes which cannot be fully realised in one daring act, since they challenge prejudices which may be among the most deeply rooted in the whole range of characteristics and reactions which make up the human personality. The role of the woman and her attitude towards the kibbutz are not only decisive because they affect half the kibbutz population. They are qualitative issues of major significance, because of their untold influence upon the education of the new generation and the character of the kibbutz family, upon both of which the kibbutz future depends so largely. In other areas, partial achievements are tolerable, but the revolution effected as regards the woman in the kibbutz must go forward constantly, and neither the woman nor kibbutz society can be satisfied with the great achievements already recorded. And it is because the vision is so revolutionary that the realisation is so problematical.

The new kibbutz-born generation has been brought up and educated to take full equality for granted, as a natural right. It will be less inhibited by the prejudices of the old society, and may therefore be less tolerant of the discrepancy between current achievements (which it will also take for granted) and the liberation of the full potential of the woman, which is the real significance of a new and equal society. For them, the real question may not be: is the woman equal? Rather, it will be: how will she use her equality?—What sort of woman will this equality breed? This question, which opens up new dimensions and new perspectives, not only for the woman but for the whole of kibbutz and socialist society, still awaits its ultimate answer.

CHAPTER 11

The New Generation

THE basic historical test of every commune, and particularly of the
kibbutz as a voluntary collective in a hostile environment, rests
with the second generation. It is they who, more than any other
single factor, will determine whether the kibbutz is an episode or a
permanent historical phenomenon.

We have seen how the birth of the kibbutz was the result of the
conscious revolt of Jewish youth against the cruel reality of the
Dispersion, the specific needs of Zionist colonisation, and the yearning for a better and juster way of life founded on labour, brotherhood, equality and justice. This unique combination of historical
circumstances, which made the foundation of the kibbutz possible,
is either wholly or partly irrelevant to the new generation born and
bred in the commune. If the kibbutz is to guarantee its historical
continuity, it must perpetuate the values on which it was founded
among a generation whose life experience has been totally different.

FATHERS AND SONS

Year by year, some 500 of these sons and daughters of the kibbutz
complete their studies, finish their army service, and return to their
settlements to take up the responsibilities of kibbutz life side by
side with their parents. In the veteran kibbutzim of Hashomer
Hatzair, they already constitute up to a half of the membership and
it will not be long before the present merging of two generations,
with all its quandaries, will give way to a kibbutz society in which
those born and bred in the new reality will become the dominant
factor in shaping the kibbutz future.

The new generation is first and foremost entirely *different* from that of the founders. For them, all the struggles of the past are no more than legends. One kibbutz veteran tells how he tried to bring home to his son what their kibbutz looked like when its slopes were bare of the thick forests which now provide blessed shelter against the burning sun; but he realised gradually that it did not matter to his son whether the trees were planted a year ago or a century ago. For him, the trees were always there, for he had grown up under their shelter. They represented the reality of his kibbutz landscape, and nothing else could ever exist in his consciousness.

Every Israeli knows that at the time of the Eichmann trial, the *Sabra* (Israel-born) generation found it wellnigh incomprehensible that six million European Jews should have been slaughtered by the Nazis, while only a handful organised armed resistance. For this youth, strong, independent and proud of its national independence, the defencelessness of the Jew in Dispersion is strange and remote. It can be explained and learned, but it is outside their life experience and alien to their psychology and make-up.

Hard as this may be, the older generation must realise that if the two generations are to conduct a dialogue rather than a monologue, to understand their children as they are and not only as they would perhaps like them to be, this must be founded on the simple and irrevocable fact that the two generations are different. All the nostalgia for the past, which is expressed in the style of "When-I-was-your-age", like the bare slopes which preceded the afforestation, are unreal and even incongruous to a generation born and bred in the commune to whom the life and ways of the Dispersion are known only from hearsay. The spiritual fabric of the kibbutz *Sabra* was woven in the homeland and in the communal village. The question is not whether he will be like his father, but whether, being different, he will nevertheless follow in his footsteps.

INFLUENCES AND PATTERNS

Three primary influences shape the character of the new generation: communal education, which sets out to educate a type of human being suited to kibbutz life in his personality and values; the kibbutz, as a reality, not only an ideal, in which the parents and the family circle are of special importance; and the values of Israeli society and those of the wide world outside, which are absorbed through literature, press and radio, film and theatre, family and friends in town, the army and a thousand other channels and sources.

It is, of course, an oversimplification to speak of kibbutz youth as a whole. The same environment produces different reactions among different individuals and if we search for a common denominator we are always in danger of overlooking that kibbutz society is made up of individuals with their own personalities and inclinations. Nevertheless, some of the questions which determine the role of the new generation in the kibbutz's quest for historical continuity already have partial answers founded upon experience with such large numbers that they appear to be generally representative of a definite pattern.

First of all, about 80 per cent of kibbutz children opt to remain in the kibbutz when they grow up. By the end of the 1960's they accounted for about a third of K.A. membership, a half of which is now under the age of 35. That the great majority chooses to stay in the kibbutz is not for lack of opportunity to make their lives elsewhere. The first prolonged meeting with the reality of outside society, which usually takes place around the age of 18 in the army, proves conclusively that their personality and education open before broad vistas of prospects for good careers.

Though only about 4 per cent of the total population, kibbutz youth makes up 22 per cent of officers in the Israel Army. Highly instructive information about kibbutz sons is contained in the results of a sociological survey conducted in the army from 1961 to 1964 by Dr. Yehuda Amir, lecturer in Psychology at the Bar-Eilan University.[*] "The kibbutz sons come to the army with basic data which gives them preference (as soldiers) over the rest of the population." A combined index of education, intelligence, knowledge of the

[*] See *Magamot*, Quarterly of the Behavioural Sciences, August 1967 (Hebrew).

Hebrew language and personal characteristics showed more than twice as many kibbutz soldiers in the top level (37: 16 per cent) and medium level (51: 24 per cent) than the rest of the population; in the medium–low level, the relationship is reversed (10: 28 per cent), while in the bottom level the figures are 2 per cent of kibbutz youth, 32 per cent of the rest.

As in other armies, three criteria are highly valued—the volunteering rate, since a readiness to do more than the minimum demanded is an important attribute; success in courses; and progress as N.C.O.s and officers.

The following table refers to the rate of volunteering:

	1 (high)	2	3	4 (low)
Kibbutz youth	30	24	23	22
Others	5	11	24	60

It is interesting to note that those not born in the kibbutzim but educated there from at least the age of 10, though in the combined index they were closer to the non-kibbutz youth, were close to the kibbutz youth in volunteeering rate and in personal suitability for the army.

In suitability for positions of command (officers) the figures are:

	High	Medium	Low
Kibbutz youth	58	18	24
Other youth	35·5	20·5	44

Twenty-eight per cent from the kibbutz passed suitability tests with high marks as against 6 per cent of the rest.

In order to make comparisons for suitability for positions of command on a uniform basis, Kibbutz youth was compared to that non-kibbutz youth similar in terms of background, education and personality. Here, too, kibbutz youth stands out:

	Kibbutz youth	Others
High	62·5	50
Medium	16·5	22·5
Low	21	27·5

In these categories, those educated in the kibbutz but not born there were more similar to the non-kibbutz youth.

Finally, the figures show that less kibbutz youth drop out of the officers' courses and their progress as officers is better than the general rate. Dr. Amir concludes that the kibbutz youth is better according to all the criteria. Why? "It may be assumed that the difference stems in some way from the framework of kibbutz life. Possibly it is connected with the way of bringing up the child or with later educational influence or maybe with group influences and social pressure to succeed in the army. . . ."

Writing in an army newspaper, one correspondent sums up that the kibbutz youth excel in the army, have won a place of honour and are respected by their commanding officers. His complaint is that after their conscription period is over, they return to the plough whereas, as Dr. Amir also concludes, "their contribution to the army is most important, vital and necessary".

Speaking to reporters, Dr. Amir assumed that both heredity and environment are at work here. The average kibbutz child enjoys a greater degree of stability, both as regards family circle and educators, in the formative years. Since education in the kibbutz is considered so important to society as a whole, the kibbutz child enjoys more prospects of getting the sort of educational environment and individual attention which he needs in order to develop personality, self-confidence and the ability to succeed.

The spirit of volunteering and pioneering makes kibbutz youth "a natural" for leadership in a land where security is so much a part of the national need, and they play a role quite out of proportion to their numbers in every military action which requires special initiative, staying-power and the readiness to make quick and independent decisions. Along with their courage and devotion, these qualities make them in demand not only in the army, but fit them to take up important positions in other spheres of Israel's dynamic development if they choose to leave the kibbutz.

That they choose to stay in the kibbutz is therefore the first and major positive achievement—and a condition of all the others. The second is that unlike their parents they are workers for whom agriculture and physical labour are natural and self-understood. They have grown up in, and feel part of, a workers' society. For their parents, the dignity of labour was a revolutionary concept accompanied by heart-searching and suffering, romanticised and idealised, the realisation of a dream and an ideology demanding a conscious and often heroic effort. For the new generation it is a fact of life accepted as such from childhood without romanticism and sentimentality. Their roots in the land and in labour are so deep that it is superfluous to make a fuss of them.

They work unaffectedly, spontaneously and instinctively. It is in their bones, and to eulogise the idea of a Jewish worker or farmer is strange to them. They are skilled agriculturalists and industrial workers who have taken over the organisation of various branches with outstanding success. This is the second great achievement of the new generation in the kibbutz.

Thirdly, their personality is attuned to the patterns of communal living, and on becoming kibbutz members, they accept the commune naturally and positively. A revolutionary concept like communal education is for them a part of the natural order of things, and where they are critical, it is flaws in the execution of the system which they criticise, and not the system as such. They want it to work better, but see it as a logical and proven method of bringing up their children. Equality, collective consumption, mutual aid, the responsibility of the group for the individual and of the individual to the group—all this is deemed right and reasonable. Far from showing tendencies to revert to a more individualistic society, they accept the superiority of the commune and are concerned not to challenge its tenets, but to improve its practical effectivity.

Fourthly, they show maturity and encouraging stability in their married life. Promiscuity is rare, and not only because public opinion frowns upon it. It seems that the free and uninhibited contact between the sexes in the children's community leads to mutual respect and to a serious approach to the establishment of a family. It makes a period of sowing one's wild oats superfluous, and precludes that sort of wild and irresponsible reaction which expresses rebellion against dual morality in bourgeois ethics. Though the general atmosphere of early marriage has its dangers, the fear that it might drive young people into hasty and incompatible marriages has not been borne out.

DEEP FURROWS

For the new generation, the kibbutz is above all a home. This is where they grew up, and deep emotional ties bind them to its landscape and changing seasons. These are the fields where they romped as children, the paths they trod, the woods where they camped out. Every corner of the farm brings back its own happy memories and childhood associations. In place of the wandering Jew, aware of the hostility of his temporary urban environment, always on the move in the search for something better and more secure, we have a generation deeply attached to the land, characterised by the stability and security of people whose two feet are firmly planted in the soil.

The normalisation of Jewish life, of which the Zionist movement always dreamed, reaches a far higher expression in the rural life of the kibbutz than in the hustle and bustle of Tel Aviv. Herzl once wrote that "when the strong hand of the Jewish peasant once more guides the plough, the Jewish problem will be solved". In this sense, the sons of the kibbutz have indeed solved the eternal problem of the wandering Jew.

Yet here, too, we can see the source of the kibbutz dilemma. For the Jewish problem is not yet solved. Israel is not only a home for its citizens, but a magnet for millions of Jews still on the move. The kibbutz is not only a home for its members, including its sons, but a collective, striving to shine out as a beacon to the society outside it. Since its whole existence is a challenge to that society, it cannot exist without special characteristics of militancy, crusading spirit, socialist consciousness and dynamic sense of mission. This is the second deep furrow which the new generation must plough. For the founding generation, the kibbutz was a historical mission, motivated by a Socialist–Zionist ideology which grew from life experience of Dispersion and Capitalism. For the new generation, the kibbutz is a fact. It is taken for granted. It is a natural and satisfying way of life.

Like their counterparts in other parts of the world, both West and East, kibbutz youth is more impressed by fact than by theory. It has little patience for phraseology and none for moralising. It is so practical that some would call it pragmatic. This down-to-earthedness accounts for its exceptional ability in practical, clearly defined tasks like raising agricultural yields. On the other hand, it is no coincidence that in modern Hebrew slang, "to preach Zionism" is a derogatory phrase with which the *Sabras* express their distaste for anything which they consider smacks of superfluous moralising.

To these general factors must be added those which particularly affected politically leftist youth. Feelings of shock and soul-searching shook the Kibbutz Artzi in the wake of the Twentieth Congress of the Soviet Communist Party. The distortions of the Stalin period, the style of the Soviet–Chinese rift and some developments in China itself—all left their mark upon a generation growing to political maturity in the 1960's and 1970's. But Israeli attitudes were shaped above all by the Soviet attitude to Zionism and especially by the U.S.S.R.'s increasing support—political and military—for the Arab States against Israel. In the Six-Day War of June 1967, Israel fought against armies equipped with the latest Soviet arms and backed to the hilt by Soviet diplomacy (the exact opposite of the position in Israel's War of Independence in 1948). Soviet prestige now sunk to its lowest point, with all the implications involved as regards the political attitudes of the young generation in the kibbutz.

MORE THAN A HOME

The great question-mark hanging over the new generation in the kibbutz is no longer whether they will take over the reins from their fathers. This they have already answered in the affirmative, firmly and capably. What remains unanswered as yet—and perhaps only the third generation can answer it—is whether they will see the kibbutz not only as a way of life but also as an instrument in the great political and social struggles of our times: whether they will feel loyalty, not only to the internal values of kibbutz life, but also to the conception of the kibbutz as a fighting vanguard of a new society. This will demand not only an emotional attachment to the kibbutz as a home for themselves and their children, but also a readiness to become personally involved in its political and ideological struggles, to strike out against hostile currents surrounding the kibbutz and threatening its existence from all sides.

If times were different, this would be an easier proposition. But the pioneering values of pre-State Israel, in which the kibbutz flourished, have given way to an atmosphere of careerism, individualism and cynicism, in which youth is encouraged to believe that it is each man for himself and the devil take the hindmost. Reliance on the all-powerful bureaucratic apparatus of the State pushed social consciousness and voluntary pioneering into the background. In this atmosphere, large sections of youth throw moral scruples to the winds and look for individual salvation in good jobs and easy living.

The kibbutz was put on the defensive by these trends. It is compelled to consolidate within its present framework instead of establishing many new settlements and so maintaining its pioneering dynamic. Yet if this was the tone of the 1950's, the kibbutz movement in the 1960's is fighting back with a renewed feeling of strength against the trend towards isolation. These external challenges have caused a certain degree of internal doubt and confusion. They emphasise the isolation both of the kibbutz and of the values for which it stands.

TESTS AND TASKS

Whenever the new kibbutz generation has been put to the test, it has proved itself. For example, it has been called upon to give what is called a "third year of service" to the Kibbutz Artzi over and above the conscription period. Hundreds of young people have been drafted to help young kibbutzim struggling to establish themselves, and kibbutz-born youth has willingly accepted this inter-kibbutz mutual aid, contributing their ability and experience freely and fully. In educational work among city youth and Jewish youth abroad, they have been tested and not found wanting. Yet it is a fact that they have generally preferred to channelise their main energy into the practical work of the farm or the children's house rather than into ideological or political work.

The farm involves practical tasks, readily understood, in which practical results can be seen. Other issues are more confusing and less clear-cut. In the army, the graduates of kibbutz high schools are suddenly confronted with a generation of town youth bent, for the most part, only upon their own careers, sometimes cynical and even scornful of the "naïve" convictions of kibbutz youth, and underlining their isolation. They come home to the kibbutz more mature but less secure, not so much cynical as questioning.

At once they must plunge into the maelstrom of kibbutz life, working a full day, accepting responsibility, settling down and establishing a family. Particularly for the girls, there is the problem of finding a satisfying place of work. The kibbutz is concerned to develop and utilise the talents of all, but it was limited by economic necessity, by the need to foster individual talents within a given framework. With comparatively few exceptions, the broad facilities which it offered for adult education were more in the nature of part-time studies than full-time attendance at university. Teaching, as a profession, offers possibilities to a certain number of the more intellectually-inclined, but candidates for such vocations as agronomy or productivity-engineering must first of all prove themselves in the daily life and work of the kibbutz. This is a principle which the kibbutz must apply equally to young and old alike.

The attitude of the kibbutzim to higher education has undergone revolutionary changes over recent years. As the settlements grow and branch out, they need more specialists and experts in all fields. They can also better afford their training. Nowadays, there is, too, a more understanding attitude to so-called "non-functional" studies. Motivated both by objective kibbutz needs for know-how, and by the inclinations of some young kibbutz members to continue studying after High school, the kibbutz movement is doing all it can to provide higher education in courses under its control in various institutions of higher learning, full as well as part-time. (In spite of a certain dissatisfaction with some aspects of existing university and college courses, the idea of a "Kibbutz College" seems premature. Many kibbutz members are studying at university.) There are indications that this trend not only to permit but even to encourage further studies will change the face of the kibbutz in years ahead. The question is no longer whether but how and when and what to learn.

In the long run, talent and a genuine desire to study will be recognised but it must as far as possible be merged with the requirements of the kibbutz. For young people with special inclinations this provides a perspective but not always an immediate answer to the problems of integration in the first and difficult years after the army.

This, then, is a period when the kibbutz is no longer only an ideal, but is revealed as a living reality with its own contradictions and dilemmas. The complaints and grumbles of the older generation are not lost upon the youth. Inevitably this is a time of tests and tension, and it is hardly surprising that the youngsters are involved above all in finding their own place and solving their own problems as, for the first time, they face the complications and pressures of adult life. Though they consciously do so within the commune and according to its ways, some complain that they lack the fervour and passion which the older generation remember from their own youth.

PARTNERSHIP OF GENERATIONS

The meeting in kibbutz life with the parent generation is not entirely free of conflict and mutual dissatisfaction. The restless energy, know-how and occasional extremism of youth come face to face with the long experience and maturity of the veterans. This complex and sensitive meeting of two generations, different yet united, demands a degree of mutual consideration which each party sometimes complains is lacking in the other.

The older generation may feel that it is being pushed out before its time, or that the youngsters show insufficient respect for their elders and for values always considered sacred. The younger generation is uncertain what specific task awaits it and may sense that it is being held back too long from exploiting its own potential for organisation and leadership. Extremes are bad counsellors here, for only a middle road satisfying the legitimate ambitions of youth without sacrificing the experience of age can serve the common interest of both generations and the objective needs of the kibbutz.

Few societies can compare with the kibbutz in the possibilities which it affords to avoid the tragedy of a war between the generations. Though they are different, there is no contradiction between their moral, cultural and social values. They are full and equal partners in a common venture. Precisely because of this common basis of aspirations, the only social values which can be transmitted from generation to generation are those which are practised, not those which are preached in theory and breached in practice.

As long as the old generation is still in its prime, the sons' integration into the kibbutz will be shaped above all by the personal example which they see around them.

They are highly adapted to take up the mission of the kibbutz, yet since they have been educated from an early age to reject sophistry and hypocrisy, they are particularly sensitive to any discrepancy between theory and practice. This is why the meeting between the generations is as much a test of the parents as of the sons. Communal education prepares the ground and sows the seeds, but they do not grow in the artificial conditions of a glasshouse. The kibbutz provides their sustenance and determines how they will blossom and flower.

The fact is that the education of kibbutz youth does not stop at the age of 18. Kibbutz schooling can do no more than prepare the younger generation to face the dilemmas of life for itself. Since there is no insuperable gulf between the generations, it has been found that this is most effectively accomplished within a separate framework (*Chativa Tseira*) for people in their 20's and 30's in which the special problems of youngsters facing the problems of integration into the broader framework can be more fully and freely expressed and clarified. The increasingly encouraging result of this innovation provide the best guarantee that the kibbutz will be able to avoid the dilemma of conservative societies whose "angry young men" flare up briefly and settle down quickly as values become conventions and independence gives way to conformism. The youth section is a bridge between communal education and kibbutz life. It prepares the children of yesterday to take their own destiny—and that of the kibbutz movement—into their own hands.

We have noted that the younger generation loves the kibbutz and cherishes its way of life. When they have been faced with real tests, be it on the field of battle or of labour, they have proved worthy of all the hopes invested in them. They are maturing at a time when the clash between the commune as a new society and those external trends and values which would isolate it and destroy it is sharpening, so that many of the major tests facing kibbutz youth still lie before it. On the basis of their past record, there is every reason to believe that the wonderful inheritance into which they were born is in faithful and worthy hands.

CHAPTER 12

Culture in the Kibbutz

ITS rich and varied intellectual life is one of the most outstanding indications that the kibbutz is not only a communal farm but a new way of life in which the highest cultural values, customarily associated with the bright lights of the big city, are brought back to the countryside and find an expression fitting to the aspirations of a new type of man for whom labour and culture go hand in hand in the building of a new society.

LABOUR AND CULTURE

In literature, art, dancing, music and drama, the kibbutzim are among the most important centres of creative culture in Israel; many of the world's greatest musicians have noted that it is a unique experience to play before a kibbutz audience; the Kibbutz Artzi owns one of Israel's largest publishing houses—the Sifriat Poalim* (Workers' Library); it is in the kibbutz that the celebration of Jewish festivals in the spirit of the new secular Hebrew renaissance

* Sifriat Poalim has published some 1000 books during the last quarter of a century. About half of these are novels, stories and poems, equally divided between original Hebrew works and translations from other languages. About 200 books deal with education and the social sciences. Other subjects include nature, art, and works of research or reference in science and the humanities. Sifriat Poalim has pioneered the translation into Hebrew of the Marxist classics. In general, the duel policy and purpose of the publishing house is to encourage original Hebrew writing, both fiction and non-fiction, and to bring the Hebrew reader translations of all that is significant in world literature with special emphasis on works of progressive social content.

150

has reached its highest expression; and the internal life of the kibbutz is characterised by a cultural level of which many urban communities would be justifiably jealous.

Superficially, it may seem incongruous that a workers' society should be able to maintain such an intensive tempo of cultural life, but on examination it would appear that it could hardly be otherwise. The intellectual level of the kibbutz population is generally extremely high, and its cultural tastes highly developed. Partly cut off from the attractions of the metropolis, its members will be condemned to a life of boredom, monotony and spiritual frustration unless the kibbutz finds ways and means to enrich their communal life with satisfying cultural content.

Of course members can and do enjoy the pleasures of literature, radio and cinema. Every kibbutz has a good library, every room its own radio, and there is a weekly film-show as well as visits to theatres and concerts in the nearest urban centre. Like cultured people everywhere, the kibbutz member may often be found relaxing after his day's work in his own room, enjoying the book or radio programme of his choice.

INDEPENDENT CREATIVITY

But there are least two reasons why, with all its importance, the kibbutz cannot exist only upon "imported" culture. First, it has cultural values of its own, which have nothing in common with much of the cheap, artificial, escapist and unaesthetic imports now flooding Israel's towns and undermining the taste of many citizens, including broad circles of its youth. Second, a society as creative, dynamic and revolutionary as the kibbutz must fight against the trend to see culture and recreation as restricted to the passive absorption of what is produced by the entertainment industry. If it is on the receiving end, without control over the choice of product, it leaves itself wide open to the destructive influences of alien concepts. It can only resist this encroachment of hostile ideas into its own camp by encouraging an independent creativity, both individual and communal, by nurturing the cultural talents and inclinations of its members so as to create a cultural image of its own, which will express its own life and outlook.

The cultural image of the kibbutz, like the kibbutz itself, is therefore of twofold importance: it is a value of its own, and it is an instrument in the projection of the kibbutz outside. It enriches the daily life of its members, but it also plays an important role as the home and concentration-point of all those circles in Israel who understand that very little culture is in fact "neutral" and that the struggle for the future image of Israel society as a whole is fought out on the cultural no less than on the political or economic front.

WHAT SORT OF CULTURE?

This is not a recent development, for the kibbutz was the cradle of most of those positive and creative values which still play a leading part in Israel's cultural life but are increasingly challenged by the Levantine atmosphere of the big cities. The kibbutz was the fountainhead of the younger generation of authors and poets, for the new folk-music and folk-dancing, art and drama of an ancient people returning to its land. The new culture, which strove to unite all that was best in Jewish tradition with the progressive universal values of modern humanism, naturally saw in the kibbutz its major inspiration. Because of its vanguard role in the national and social renaissance of Israel, the cultural impact of the kibbutz has always been quite out of proportion to its numerical importance. This cannot be attributed only to the influence of the many creative artists who are themselves members of the kibbutz. Around the values of the kibbutz and not only from within it, the most progressive and dynamic aspects of modern Hebrew culture crystallise and search for expression.

There is hardly an evening in the kibbutz without some form of cultural activity, mainly in the framework of special-interest circles far too varied to be enumerated here. Nearly every settlement has its own choir, orchestra, dramatic and folk-dancing circles, which reach exceptionally high performance standards. There are weekly or monthly bulletins and papers. Visiting lecturers, from the kibbutzim and outside, cover almost every topic under the sun. Study-circles, generally led by a kibbutz member, devote themselves to topics which range from kibbutz theory to ancient and modern Jewish and general history, Marxism and sociology, literature and mathematics, education and philosophy, the Hebrew language and economics, Arabic and English, science and archaeology.

Givat Chaviva, the central study institute of the Kibbutz Artzi, is a sort of people's university, where every member has an opportunity to learn general ideological topics and other subjects in which he shows special interest, at courses ranging from a week to a year. This is where the cultural and ideological values of the kibbutz and its techniques are systematically studied and taught, so that it has become a thriving centre of higher education, steeped in kibbutz tradition and experience.* Though each kibbutz directs its own cultural life, local specialists in every sphere are linked to national kibbutz organisations: the combined kibbutz symphony orchestra and choir, circles of photographers and archaeologists, folk-dancers and sociologists, naturalists and even chess-players, which provide impetus to local circles and enlarge their horizons and possibilities of advancement. Wherever possible there is also a high degree of regional co-operation and many areas have their own amphitheatres and even concert-halls which can afford to bring established theatres and international artists to the kibbutz.

The whole kibbutz gathers to celebrate weddings and anniversaries, the Sabbath and festivals. These provide a forum for the expression of local talent, including that of the high school children. The kibbutz audience is critical as well as appreciative, and much study is being given to the content and organisation of these evenings in order to assure that they avoid the ever-present dangers of repetition and lack of imagination. Since they bring together all the generations of the kibbutz, they are important socially as well as culturally. Nowadays many kibbutzim are also introducing regular club-evenings in the cultural centre, where members can get together

---

* Givat Chaviva has recently opened an Afro-Asian Institute where the main emphasis is on Arab studies. Many Israeli Arabs are studying at the Institute.

informally over a cup of coffee, and this innovation seems to meet a need not satisfied by larger and formal get-togethers. Particularly in younger kibbutzim, both the smaller numerical framework and a certain lack of talent and leadership make it no easy job to organise the cultural life of the kibbutz on a sufficiently high level, and this is not without its negative effects on the whole social fabric of the kibbutz.

Even so, the activisation of local talent and the appearances of outside artists and lecturers provide every kibbutz with such an intensive cultural and social life that in this respect it has nothing whatsoever in common with the traditional village. Strangers find it hard to believe that all this can be achieved by men and women working a full day in the fields or the services. The question for the kibbutz member is not so much how to avoid boredom as how to summon up the energy after a long and tiring day to exploit the cultural facilities which the kibbutz offers. Unless the cultural activities are dynamic and interesting, kibbutz members prefer to relax in their own family or social circle, following their own tastes and hobbies. Sport and athletics are highly popular, and in some branches kibbutz teams, wearing the colours of Hapoel, the Histadrut sport organisation, set the pace for the whole country.

The weekly schedule of evening activities during the cooler months of the year might be something like this: Saturday, members' meeting; Sunday, study circles; Monday, rehearsals of the choir, drama circle, orchestra, etc.; Tuesday, a film; Wednesday, a visiting lecturer; Thursday, committee meetings; Friday, *Erev Shabbat* (Sabbath eve) celebrations.

Three of these activities cater for the whole population, the others for interest-groups. In fact, this is an incomplete picture even of the organised activity going on of an evening, for those who are presenting something on Friday evening (perhaps dances, a speaking choir or a humorous skit) will also be preparing together. Neither does it take into account archaeologists, photographers and stamp-collectors who may be at work together. On the other hand, we have noted that in fact, there are those who do not always attend the members' meeting, and few lecturers draw the whole adult population into the dining-hall or cultural centre.

What with work, children and tasks in the kibbutz, members have little enough spare time. Though it is hard for them to drop into the local cinema and television is still in its infancy in Israel, they are also prey to the empty temptations of mass-communications. Unless the kibbutz can provide alternatives—and much depends on the initiative of the local cultural committee—the hours of relaxation will be dominated by a type of spiritual content which can only weaken their identification with the kibbutz. Though the "cultural consciousness" of kibbutzim varies, the whole movement is becoming increasingly aware that the cultural committee is one of the most important of all the bodies whose effectivity shapes the character and image of kibbutz life. This is reflected in the work of the Cultural Department of the Kibbutz Artzi, whose activities are among the most comprehensive of all the central bodies of the movement.

FESTIVALS

The highlights of the year in the cultural life of the kibbutz are associated with the Jewish festivals, and volumes have been written about the rich and original forms and content with which the settlements have revived their celebration. For the festivals provide unique possibilities to express the renaissance which enables Jewish farmers to celebrate the joys of harvest and of the first-fruits, of spring and redemption, after generations of exile and suffering. This merging of old and the new, of the love for land and freedom which saturates Jewish history, finds a different expression in each of the festivals which enrich Jewish tradition.

Song and dance, drama and readings, colourful pageantry and solemn remembrance blend together to give each festival its special content and atmosphere. Many are celebrated in the open air in the same landscape and language in which our forefathers gathered their own harvest. Thousands of visitors and tourists join the settlers on these occasions, for in New York, or even in Tel Aviv, the atmosphere of the kibbutz festival can be copied, but not re-created.

CREATIVE ARTISTS

Some of Israel's best-known creative artists are members of the kibbutzim, and every effort has always been made to provide members showing special promise with the time and conditions which will enable them to develop their talent. Nevertheless, the path of the kibbutz artist is not strewn with roses, for he must prove himself day by day as a member of the kibbutz and not only as an artist. As such, he enjoys the privileges but must accept the obligations of membership, and this in a society where commercial success is no criterion and where there is no special status attached to intellectual, as against physical, work.

In consultation with the appropriate section of the Cultural Department of the Kibbutz Artzi, artists, sculptors, composers, writers, poets, producers, photographers, etc., are partially (and in some special cases, wholly) released from other work in order to pursue their creative vocations, including suitable studies in Israel and abroad. The creative artist in the kibbutz is above all a member of the collective. From it he receives his inspiration to create, and his work must be loyal to its spirit and values. He must be a partner, sharing the struggles and conflicts, the joys and sadness, the light and shadow of its life. An artist who seeks "freedom" from social responsibility will not find his place in the kibbutz, but he who is of the kibbutz and not only in it finds in this identification a source of creativity rather than a limitation.

He can write or paint freely and honestly, subordinate neither to the dictates of commercialism nor to the demands of a commissar. The tremendous influence of these creative artists on the whole of Israel's cultural life, whether it be in literature or theatre, art or folklore, is the highest tribute to the inspiration which they have derived from their kibbutz life and which they have given back to it in full measure.

A FIGHTING ALTERNATIVE

In pre-State Israel, all men of foresight knew that the brightest lights shone from the watchtowers of pioneering workers' settlements, and that the city lights shone dimly in comparison. The decline in pioneering values and the increasing social differentiation which have come with statehood and mass immigration, much of it from under-developed countries, have been accompanied by deep changes in social values and cultural patterns. The neon lights of the city illuminate a new petty-bourgeois style of living for some, and a hitherto unknown cultural wilderness for the under-priviliged. On the one hand, the stifling blanket of orthodox religion would have the whole population live according to the reactionary laws of medieval clericalism. Side by side with this, there is a growth of snobbery and cheap imitation, form without content, technique without values, the noisy emptiness of the night-club and the sexy vulgarity of the Hollywood-style bar. This atmosphere retards the process of the merging of the ethnic groups and the crystallisation of an original and indigenous Hebrew culture.

The kibbutz stands out in sharp contrast to these dangerous trends. It does not stand alone, for wide circles are beginning to understand that the growth of juvenile delinquency in this milieu is not coincidental. But it is a rallying point for all those who are searching for progressive secular cultural patterns, for an original Hebrew culture and style of life, conduct, dress, recreation, mores and outlook. It presents a fighting alternative, a living proof that labour and creative culture can be integrated, that the ethnic groups can be united, that working youth must not of necessity be condemned to a life of pseudo-sophistication and spiritual frustration. This is one of the most important contributions of the kibbutz to the broad struggle for the future image of Israel society.

CHAPTER 13

The Kibbutz Artzi as a Movement

THE Kibbutz Artzi is a national movement rather than a federation of autonomous settlements. Through its democratically elected institutions it clarifies and determines general principles and practical policies in every sphere of kibbutz life. It is responsible for inter-kibbutz mutual aid, for the allocation of manpower resources available to the settlements, and for representation of the kibbutzim in national bodies—government agencies, the Histadrut and the Zionist institutions. It is responsible for the Hashomer Hatzair youth movement in Israel and abroad. Though it is not a political party, it plays a leading role in the work of the United Workers' Party, Mapam, and normally provides about a hundred full-time party workers. (This is, of course, apart from the countless members of kibbutzim whose work for Mapam is carried out in neighbouring villages and towns after their day's work in the kibbutz.)

The K.A. puts out its own publications,* controls the central

* Of special importance is the weekly *Ha'shavua Bakibbutz Haartzi* ("The Week in the K.A.") which provides information about the kibbutzim taken partly from internal kibbutz bulletins, and provides a forum for the exchange of ideas and experience between kibbutz members; and the quarterly magazine *Hedim* ("Echoes") which carries more fundamental articles by members on every facet of kibbutz life and theory. It has also a section for creative writing —stories, poems, etc. *Ofakim* ("Horizons") is a magazine put out by the Educational Department and directed primarily to teachers and educationalists both in the settlements and outside them. Other Departments publish various bulletins relating to their own area of work. A recent innovation in kibbutz literature is a joint paper put out by all the kibbutz movements together. All the publications mentioned, as well as many others which we have not detailed, are attractively prepared, and illustrated by kibbutz artists. Literature in foreign languages is put out for the various branches of the world movement.

study institute at Givat Chaviva, and is a partner in the joint teachers' training colleges of the three major kibbutz movements. The activities of the K.A., which are primarily administered from its central offices in Tel Aviv, are financed by an internal system of taxation of the kibbutzim.

On a small scale, the administrative machinery of the K.A. is comparable to that of a self-governing state. Yet of the 500-odd kibbutz members who are its full-time officials, only about twenty remain in office permanently. Every kibbutz must provide about 6 per cent of its members for central movement work, and about two-thirds of these are replaced every two years. Since the movement is interested in the services of the most able kibbutz members —those whom it is hardest for the kibbutz to release—their mobilisation is no easy matter. Here, as in general in kibbutz life, mutual persuasion and negotiation are preferred to administrative decrees.

The movement is prepared to go to almost any lengths to clarify, to explain and to convince a kibbutz why a particular step is deemed essential. Though differences of opinion between kibbutz and movement are common, mutual confidence and internal movement responsibility usually prevail in the end. This does not preclude occasional clashes and friction on delicate and vital problems like the allocation of manpower or the release of a member for movement or party work. Where it is felt that a matter of basic principle is at stake, the institutions of the movement have the ultimate right to enforce movement discipline. But this is rare, and in general the fundamental identity of interests makes it possible to avoid head-on clashes. It must be remembered that, as in the kibbutz, the system of rotating tasks makes the development of a central movement bureaucracy impossible, and today's movement representative is a rank-and-file kibbutz member tomorrow.

DEPARTMENTS

Very few major decisions in the kibbutz are made without consultation with the appropriate Department of the Kibbutz Artzi, and no less than twenty Departments,* with their own subsections, advise the kibbutzim, centralise their experience, and serve those individuals and committees responsible for a particular area of kibbutz life. In order to illustrate how these Departments function, we might look, for example, at the work undertaken by the Department for Social Affairs. With a staff of seven or eight full-time workers, it is responsible for maintaining contact with the secretary and social committee in each kibbutz.

It visits the kibbutzim, especially the younger ones, regularly, and when necessary appears before the Secretariat or the general assembly. It deals with all the social aspects of kibbutz life and lays down standards and norms for their regulation—equality, democracy, collective consumption, the woman in the kibbutz, etc. It recommends to the Secretariat of the Kibbutz Artzi, of which its central organiser is a member, plans for the allocation of manpower, which means that it must have intimate knowledge of both the manpower and the social composition and problems of every settlement. It is responsible for new groups from the movement undergoing a preparation-period before joining a kibbutz permanently, including the choice of the kibbutz where they will train, and for such groups in the army. It is also responsible for temporary help to young kibbutzim—work-camps, the mobilisation of the sons of older kibbutzim for a "third year of service" to the movement after army-service, emergency help, etc.

It convenes regular seminars and study-courses for the secretaries and chairmen of the social committees in the kibbutzim, and initiates basic discussions of outstanding questions in the central institutions of the movement: the *Moetza* (about 500 representatives of all the kibbutzim, meets yearly); the *Vaad Poel* (about 150 members, meets every 2 months); the *Maskirut* (13 members, meets weekly).

---

* These include: Youth Aliya, absorption, health, education, economic affairs, industry, mechanisation, central buying, finance, insurance, culture, political activity, agricultural planning and research, building, electricity, water, security, the Hashomer Hatzair youth movement in Israel and abroad, personnel, social affairs, youth section. In many areas. there is a high degree of co-operation with parallel Departments of the other kibbutz movements.

The Social Department also receives individual members of the kibbutzim, in order to advise them on special personal problems. This glimpse at the work of one Department can give some indication of the comprehensive scope of the work of all of them.

POOLING EXPERIENCE

The Kibbutz Artzi is deeply involved in the practical everyday problems of kibbutz life, but its real significance as a movement lies in its ability to ensure that every problem, small and large, of the individual kibbutz will be approached in the light of the guiding principles of the whole movement. It is far harder for an individual kibbutz than it is for the movement as a whole, to see the relationship of a particular problem, economic or social, cultural or educational, to broad principles. Under the harsh pressure of circumstances, an individual kibbutz tackling a problem (like hired labour) always faces the danger that it will beat what looks like a temporary retreat from an accepted principle.

From its vantage-point surveying the whole map of the Kibbutz Artzi, the movement is better able to place what appears like a local problem in its correct relationship to universal values. It can show how an accumulation of temporary retreats can threaten values on a broad front, and how other kibbutzim in similar circumstances managed to avoid this danger. Through the movement, one kibbutz can draw conclusions of its own from the successes and failures of another. It is hard to imagine the functioning of any kibbutz without the untold advantages which all derive from this pooling of experience.

The principle of mutual aid between the kibbutzim of Hashomer Hatzair has nowhere been more radically or successfully expressed than in the mobilisation of the sons of veteran kibbutzim for a "third year of service" over and above the regular army conscription period. The idea was first broached when it became clear that because of the lack of manpower reserves which became apparent in the 1950's, many of the kibbutzim established after 1948, most of them border-settlements, were not strong enough to overcome their problems without help from outside.

The basic solution lay, of course, in the reinforcement of these struggling settlements with pioneering groups from the youth movement in Israel and abroad. However, such groups were too few in number to answer all the pressing needs in time; meanwhile, there was a danger that the whole unstable structure of the young Kibbutzum struggling with too few members against grave economic, social and security problems, would be undermined.

The Executive Council of the K.A. proposed to the movement a comprehensive plan whereby a veteran kibbutz would "adopt" a younger one. It would provide expert guidance both in agricultural branches and the services, and in social affairs. Year by year, a group of army-returnees from the veteran settlement (a fixed percentage according to the numbers released from the army every year, including both men and women and young families) would go to live and work in the young kibbutz. This was a heavy burden for kibbutzim which had been waiting for years for the new blood provided by their grown-up sons and daughters, and there is no surplus of manpower in veteran settlements whose founder-members are already over 50 years old.

Yet once the whole movement was persuaded that for some young kibbutzim this "blood-transfusion" was a matter of life and death, the principle of a third year of service was accepted and the plan carried out to the full in spite of the conscious sacrifice it entailed for the veteran settlements. The experiment worked out even better than originally anticipated, and to the benefit of both parties.

The members of the young kibbutzim not only received a new lease of life in their economic, social and cultural endeavours, but this in turn strengthened their weakened morale and did away with the feeling that they were being left to their fate, as it were. This stemmed the tendency in some young settlements for members to give up what looked like an unequal struggle and leave the kibbutz because they felt that there were no better perspectives for the future.

In addition, this test also had salutary effects for the sons and daughters of the older kibbutzim, broadening their horizons, strengthening their independence and deepening their feeling of identification with the movement as a whole. Many of the younger kibbutzim have meanwhile received the long-awaited reinforcements and can face their future with a new confidence. This would have been impossible without the help received during the harsh transition period, and the K.A. can sum up with justified pride this translation into practical action of the principle of mutual aid within its kibbutzim.

Even so there still remain kibbutzim of the K.A. struggling to reach the sort of viable economic, social and educational framework which cannot be achieved without at least 100 members. A glance at the figures on pp. 200–1 show that though the kibbutz population grows year by year, it cannot, as a selective society, keep pace with the growth-rate of Israel's Jewish population during periods of mass immigration. Of all the problems facing the kibbutz movement, none is more decisive than that of speeding up the rate of growth of the kibbutzim.

In the years 1955–65, the annual rate of growth for the kibbutz population has been about 1 per cent. This compares with 4 per cent for the Jewish population. Calculations show that were this trend to continue, the kibbutz share in the population would drop to some 2 per cent of Israel's Jewish total by the 1980's. This assumes a continued large immigration—in the decade from 1955 the average was about 46,000 but it fell drastically in 1966–7.

In 1960–5, 30 per cent of the population growth in the K.A. came from its own sons and daughters joining the kibbutzim; 15 per cent from Youth Aliya and outside children in kibbutz schools; 33 per cent from Hasomer Hatzair (15 per cent from abroad, 18 from Israel); and the remaining 22 per cent from other categories—individuals and families, people who married kibbutz members, etc.

Yet it must not be forgotten that in a voluntary society like the kibbutz, there are also those who leave the settlements and the overall rate of growth is determined by the ratio of these joining to those leaving the kibbutz. The percentage of members leaving the K.A. reached 9·7 per cent of total membership in 1949, fell gradually to 3·7 in 1956, rose to about 6 in 1957–9 and has been going down since then to the 1965 figure of 3·1 (388 members; of candidates—7·9 per cent). However, this burden is not divided equally—on the contrary, the larger and stronger kibbutz may have a higher potential for absorbing and integrating newcomers than the smaller and weaker settlement. In this, as in other areas, kibbutzim differ from each other. The K.A. has an overall responsibility to raise all its kibbutzim to the viability level. The special problem of those kibbutzim which are still unconsolidated, though they grow fewer in number year by year, is still in the centre of the movement's obligations.

No written constitution lays down strict limits between the autonomy of the individual kibbutz and the authority of the K.A. as a movement. The K.A. is known as the most highly centralised and disciplined of all the kibbutz movements. Critics see what they call its "clannishness" as a defect, but within its ranks there is no shadow of doubt that the highly developed sense of unity binding together its kibbutzim is one of its prime sources of strength.

Perhaps it is no coincidence that the K.A. often speaks of itself as a family, for this comes closest to expressing its sense of kinship, founded in common origins and ideals, and expressed through maximum mutual aid and common responsibility in their pursuit.

PART 3

PERSPECTIVES

There was an historical situation of a people visited by a great internal revolution. Further, this historical situation threw up an élite—the chalutzim or pioneers—drawn from all classes of the people and thus beyond class. The form of life that befitted this élite was the rural collective . . . in which the social ideal could materially influence the national idea. As the historical conditions have shown, it was impossible for this élite and the form of life it favoured to become static or isolated. The pioneer spirit is, in every part, related to the growth of a new and transformed national community; the moment it grew complacent it would have lost its soul. . . . The dynamics of history determined the dynamic character of the relations between the rural collective and society as a whole.

MARTIN BUBER, *Paths in Utopia*

Not only in Israel, but in every country in which a new society is being built, I see in pioneering and revolutionary volunteering the peak of socialist democracy in consummation.

From the history of the kibbutz movement in our country we have learned that thanks to this revolutionary pioneering force it was possible even in a non-Socialist State like ours to establish a communal society on the highest standard ever attained by humanity.

This volunteering is incomparably stronger than any extraneous discipline. This is what gave the Israel army its great advantage, what brought about the comradeship in arms between officers and men to which we were witness during the Six Day War. This pioneering voluntarism constitutes the highest peak which democracy is capable of reaching. From this point of view, the kibbutz movement can serve as an example not only for our country but for every social and national liberation movement the world over.

MEIR YAARI, theses towards the Fifth Convention of Mapam, 1968

ISRAEL was not created in 1948 primarily for those Jews who were then its citizens, for Jewish Statehood has no historical significance or justification except as the focal point for the territorial concentration of the Jewish people in its historical homeland, and the creation within it of a normal, homogeneous and healthy working people.

Two decades of Jewish national independence and political sovereignty have given birth to many magnificent achievements. The Jewish population has been trebled, and a million and a quarter immigrants from 100 lands have been absorbed into the growing economy. Large tracts of desert and wilderness have been conquered in a constructive upsurge which is transforming the physical and human landscape of much of the country.

THE SIGNIFICANCE OF STATEHOOD

Yet, notwithstanding these great strides forward, over 80 per cent of the Jewish people still remains in the Dispersion, and about the same percentage of the physical area of Israel remains unpopulated. The construction of a viable economy and the winning of economic independence remain distant goals, in spite of generous external aid, particularly from world Jewry. The ethnic groups, as distant from each other as East from West, have yet to be merged and united. And the State is still surrounded by hostile neighbours who do not conceal their opposition to its very existence and wait for the day of revenge after their defeats in 1948, 1956 and 1967.

It is this glaring discrepancy between the scale of the achievements, which we would be the last to minimise, and the scope of the historical tasks still unperformed in the State of Israel, which make it imperative to reject as an optical illusion the idea that Jewish Statehood automatically provides in itself an answer to the problems which it arose to solve. It is no more than a unique historical opportunity, which can be used or misused, exploited or frittered away. It represents an outstanding achievement on the road to the full national and social liberation of the Jewish people: yet it is a turning-point rather than the end of the road, a significant milestone rather than a destination-point.

Israel at the end of the 1960's is a fascinating land of contrasts and contradictions. Constantly evolving and growing under the impact of mass immigration, it is a society in an interminable state of change, flux and movement. Everything happens "for the first time in 2000 years". Almost nothing is crystallised or stable or immutable. Hardly more than a third of its Jewish population was born within its borders, yet this old–new nation of former middle-men and merchants, intellectuals and professionals, tradesmen and tailors can no longer rely on others to produce its daily bread.

They themselves must become farmers and industrial workers, miners and fishermen. A nation of traditional town and city-dwellers must redeem the wastelands and populate the country-side. Much has been started, but very little has been completed. The image of the nation, the character and values of society, the economic, political, and cultural content of Jewish independence—all these are in various stages of crystallisation, and the end-result has yet to be determined.

THE STATE AS A CULT

In pre-State Israel we have noted that the Jewish population was mobilised of its own free will in the struggle for immigration, colonisation, defence and political independence. This was a vast voluntary effort, directed by voluntary organisations such as the Zionist institutions, the Histadrut and the Haganah (defence-force). The kibbutz movement was the pioneer of this effort, and because it was able to accept the major burdens and sacrifices, the kibbutz member was the cream of society and his pioneering example an inspiration to all. Yet it should be remembered that the kibbutz was always a tiny minority, and well over 90 per cent of the population lived outside its communal framework even in its greatest days.

During the years of statehood, strong forces in Israel, led by the left-of-centre Mapai, the largest party in the government and in the Histadrut, increasingly fell prey to the illusion that the state machine is all-powerful. The State became the be-all and end-all of our national life and every problem could be solved by the state apparatus. Bureaucratic decrees would make superfluous the voluntary effort which was the main factor in the struggle for the creation of the State. Voluntary social forces were looked upon as an anachronism and state authority could perform their functions more effectively.

Like a wanderer in the desert who finds water and cannot stop gulping it down, state power went to the head of such veteran leaders as David Ben-Gurion, the charismatic leader who himself had been in the forefront of the pre-State voluntary forces. Younger politicians, who had risen to prominence in and around the army (Moshe Dayan, Shimon Peres), added new dimensions of pragmatism and militarism to the cult of the State. The mass immigration, much of it from backward countries lacking voluntary traditions, gave new impetus to the *étatist* conception.

For some, like Ben-Gurion, the cult of the State (*Mamlachtiut* in Hebrew) led to the rejection of all "isms" including Socialism. Even the moderate middle-of-the-road Labour-style welfare policies adopted by his successor, Levi Eshkol, were "anachronistic" for B.G. and his faction, called Rafi, which left Mapai in 1965 over clashes of personality as much as ideology. Rafi was in opposition to the Eshkol government up to the outbreak of the Six-Day War of 1967, when a wall-to-wall national government was formed.

Mapai and the more Leftish Achdut Avodah moved closer together until a united Labour party including Rafi as well was formed early in 1968. The creation of Rafi, a party born within the Israel Labour movement yet in many respects opposed to its basic tenets, showed the stresses to which the movement is subject and it remains to be seen in which direction a united Labour party including Rafi will develop.

LIP SERVICE

A right-wing government might have dared to launch an open frontal attack upon the kibbutz, but Israel's coalition governments have always been dominated by Mapai, traditionally a working-class party. Dominating the organs of state power at every level, it has always equated its own party interests with those of the State and the Histadrut. The indispensability of the kibbutz in colonisation, agriculture and defence was common knowledge, particularly in the labour movement. Though a minority in the party, Mapai's own kibbutz movement was a factor to be reckoned with.

The result was that the Israeli "establishment" spoke with several voices about the kibbutz. For managerial bureaucrats, warriors of private enterprise and the rising technocracy which flourished within the state machinery, kibbutz values were a spanner in the gears—as they had always been to capitalist circles for whom every manifestation of militant working-class independence was anathema. Within Mapai, it is customary to pay lip-service to the kibbutz. Yet Mapai's own economic and social policies increasingly undermined kibbutz values, transforming the collectives into a symbol of the past rather than a pointer to the future of Israel.

In the construction of Israeli society—in terms of values the kibbutz was levered out of the dominant position it held before the State, and relegated to playing a tolerated, but secondary role in the new scheme of things. Israeli youth must worship at the new temple of the State (which is "above class") rather than at the "narrow" shrine of voluntarism, social idealism and egalitarianism. Yet it is no coincidence that for visitors from abroad, and particularly from newly independent states striving to learn from Israel's experience, the kibbutz is still the most important showpiece of the labour movement. It is shown off proudly as the pinnacle of pioneering achievement—and some remark bitterly that those who have done so much to undermine its future present it like a quaint musket in a modern museum, valuable for export, but out of date for Israel.

What are the new weapons with which the old are to be replaced?

Leaving aside messianic phraseology, quotations from the Hebrew prophets and empty talk of "original Hebrew Socialism", the basic direction is to *capitalist "normalisation" within an all-powerful welfare-state*. The whole essence of the kibbutz interferes with this conception. The problem is that these policies are not *only* to the detriment of the kibbutz and of the young Israel working class: *they are also incapable of solving the basic problems of the State of Israel as we have defined them in their Zionist context, as a base for the absorption of the mass immigration and the normalisation of the economic and social structure of the Jewish people returning to its homeland. They answer the needs neither of social nor of national liberation.*

Three brief illustrations will serve to clarify this assumption.

PRODUCTIVISATION

1. The occupational structure of the Jewish population cannot be normalised and productivisation forwarded by these policies. Only 37·5 per cent is engaged in productive work (agriculture and industry) which is among the lowest ratios in the world. On the other hand, nearly 30 per cent is engaged in services, which is among the highest percentages in the world (15–21 per cent for Austria, Sweden, France, Switzerland and Holland, 25 per cent for England).

2. Israel has a doctor for every 420 souls, against one for 550 in the U.S.S.R., 790 in the U.S.A., and 1,100 in Sweden. Israel also has the highest proportion of people working in the free professions—nearly 12 per cent, against 9 per cent in the U.S.S.R. and 7 per cent in the U.S.A.

3. For a country hampered with limited natural resources, this top-heavy distribution is an intolerable economic burden—and the productive sector has been diminishing, rather than growing, in recent years. The economic anomaly of the Dispersion is in danger of being re-established on the soil of the homeland. Productivisation cannot be achieved by so-called "liberalisation" which means giving more freedom to the chaotic processes of capitalist economy. Between 1960 and 1965, wages in services rose by $7\frac{1}{2}$ per cent as against $3\frac{1}{2}$ per cent in productive branches. Only a

different regime based upon socialist planning, the deepening of the productive base in the economy and the encouragement of voluntary idealism—best exemplified by the kibbutz—can change the situation. This is the alternative political and social programme of Mapam to the present regime.

POLARISATION

Side by side with this structural defect in Israel's young economy, economic and social differentiation are growing, both within the working class and between the workers and the bourgeoisie. Official Finance Ministry statistics show that at the time of the establishment of the State in 1948, *net income differentiation between wage-earners stood at the ratio of 1 : 2·5. Today it is 1:7·7* (1 : 9·5 before reducing income-tax). However, even this degree of polarisation does not show the real picture because it is the lower-paid workers (mainly of Eastern origin) who support the largest families while those in the upper income-brackets have fewer children and dependants.

Looking at the extremes, we see that the 13 per cent at the bottom earning less than I£400 per month receive 4·5 per cent of the national pie while at the top, 10 per cent earning I£1450 or more received 26·6 per cent. Even moving up the scale, as against this 26·6 per cent earned by the richest one-tenth—five-tenths at the bottom received 24·4 per cent. In other words, in 1966, 10 per cent of the well-to-do earned the same as 45 per cent of poorer people. In 1961 the lower 40 per cent received a total of 16 per cent of the national income while the top 60 per cent got 84 per cent.

In equality of income distribution, Israel stands together with Britain and behind Sweden. However, it is the trend which is disturbing: while the share of the top 10 per cent in Britain's national income went down from 30 per cent in 1952 to 28 per cent in 1963, in Israel it went up from 17·7 to 26·7 per cent and is probably still rising. The trend in Western countries is towards less inequality, in Israel towards more.

We have noted that Israel is a land of contrasts—in its landscape, climate, its differing cultures and ethnic make-up. Unfortunately, it is becoming a land of social contrasts as well. In 1964 employers and self-employed made up 30 per cent of bread-winners yet they received 52 per cent of the national income. If one remembers the small self-employed farmer, craftsman, tradesman, professional and so on, one is left with a picture of ever-concentrated wealth in a small section of the population—including some 2000 home-grown Israeli millionaires—on the one hand, and some 130,000 families of slum-dwellers on the other. The welfare-state alleviates some of the cruellest hardship inherent in this capitalistic structure but no more than that.

In a land of expansion and development which should encourage the productive and pioneering elements, industrial and agricultural wages are often frozen while phenomenal profits are made by unproductive undertakings in real estate, banking, trade, commerce, finance and currency deals. While the top crust lives a life of luxury and waste, the lower-paid workers suffer austerity.

The further away one can get from productive physical work, the better the chances for affluence and prestige. In a country whose pre-State values were egalitarian, the flight from the working class has become a condition of "success". At first, careerism sought justification in the national need for experts and know-how. Nowadays such camouflage is superfluous. Prestige and affluence are no longer connected with some special contribution to the development of the country, but become independent criteria. It is not only the status and pride in his labour of the kibbutz member which has been damaged by the new wave, but all the productive sectors in the national economy. This is the price of the increasing social differentiation which is an integral part of capitalist "normalisation".

COMMUNITY INTEGRATION

The main victims of the polarisation are Oriental immigrants whose background and lack of know-how inevitably forced them into lower-paid jobs. In 1948, if the average wage of the European and Israel-born sections was 100 points, that of Jews of Oriental origin was 88. Today it is 68, a decline of 20 per cent. Here, too, one must remember the much larger Oriental family. *The net average income of the Eastern Jews is today 44 per cent that of the European and American Jews and after taxation it is still less than a half.* Gross monthly income in towns in 1964 *per soul* was I£177 for Ashkenazim, I£96 for Sephardim.

In terms of occupational distribution, only 12·6 per cent of the Eastern Jews, who make up half the population, are in the free professions, 20 per cent managers and officials. In the five top grades of the civil service they account for 5·4 per cent, going up to 39 per cent in the bottom 5 gradings. They are most highly represented in the unskilled and badly paid jobs.

These figures should not be construed as meaning that the Eastern communities are not advancing. In 1958 only 8·2 per cent of them owned an electric refrigerator. In 1965 the figure was 66·9 per cent—and this is characteristic for other household appliances as well. Even in housing, an area in which the Eastern immigrants suffer particularly because of their low income and large families, there has been vast improvement. Whereas in 1957 in 55·4 per cent of immigrant housing there were over three people to a room, the figure had gone down to 31·1 per cent by 1965.

One of the keys to the future relationship of the different ethnic groups is, of course, education. Here the figures are as follows:

In grade 1 children of Eastern communities make up 61 per cent of pupils

In grade 8 children of Eastern communities make up 45·5 per cent of pupils

In grade 12 children of Eastern communities make up 18·1 per cent of pupils

In Universities children of Eastern communities make up 17·7 per cent of students.

Here, too, there are important achievements to record. Illiteracy has been cut by half in ten years. Nearly all the children finish primary school. The proportion of Oriental students at college and university is rising—from 228 in 1957 to 2409 in 1965. Behind the figures, there is progress in absolute terms yet the relative position of the communities shows small change. The family from the Eastern countries often finds itself in a vicious circle of backwardness, poor job-opportunities, bad housing and unfinished or inferior education for the children. Those who think that time will solve the problem delude themselves.

In the development towns, where 80 per cent of the population are from the East and a third of the families are supported by welfare, elementary education is sometimes so bad that many of the children finish school barely literate. The same pattern is repeated in city slums. In a rat-race for affluence, there is little room at the top for late-starters. The enemy is social-economic and not ethnic discrimination, but, unless there will be radical changes, too many Israelis of Eastern origin could be doomed to a fate of "hewers of wood and drawers of water" in a regime where nobody need starve but the rich may get richer and the poor stay where they are. This is a perspective dangerously loaded with ethnic as well as social dynamite for Israeli society.

BOOM AND RECESSION

In the economic sphere, the first fifteen years of Israel's statehood saw the country passing from the austerity of the first years into a period of boom conditions. There was work for all. Tens of thousands of immigrants poured into the country, trebling the population between 1948 and 1965. The G.N.P. enjoyed an annual yearly growth of 11·4 per cent, among the highest in the world. Building and development flourished.

Over eighteen years, Israel received from abroad the sum of six milliard dollars in various types of financial help including American aid and German reparation money, but mostly from world Jewry. Two-thirds was in the form of grants and contributions which did not have to be repaid. If in terms of aid per head this was something of a world record, so were the dimensions of the immigration and the burden of a security budget which

T.K.—G

increased by fourteen times between 1955 and 1965 and eats away a large part of the nation's resources.

In 1966–7 the bubble burst and the artificial nature of the boom became clear to all. The balance of payments deficit was growing ominously, reaching over fifty million dollars by 1964, yet most of Israel's industry, which had grown in hothouse conditions, was incapable of competing for foreign markets. Outside aid was dropping with the completion of the German reparation agreement. Worst of all, the immigration rate slowed down and the stream looked as if it might become a mere trickle. "Emergency" immigration—that which came out of a feeling of no choice—was declining and the focus moved over to countries where the Jews lived freely, with no external stresses pushing them towards Israel. (The future of Soviet Jewry is outside the scope of this book.)

The economy slowed down. The G.N.P. increased by only 1·2 per cent in 1966. The immediate result of the recession was a quick rise in the number of unemployed. Tens of thousands found themselves out of work. At the time of writing (early 1968) the situation has improved but it is uncertain whether this was a phase which government economic policy can overcome, or the mark of a much deeper *structural* crisis with alarming implications for the future of Israeli society.

Israel cannot afford a crisis of faith in her future among her people. As a new and daring historical phenomenon—some still prefer to call it an experiment and experiments have been known to fail—Israel must inspire confidence among her own citizens, old and new. Otherwise, she has small prospects of inducing materially comfortable Jews from the West to seek a new life in the Jewish State. Leaving aside "catastrophic" immigration, which has been dominant during Israel's first two decades, there is an inescapable connection between the major patterns in Israel society and the country's drawing-power for Jews abroad who may consider immigration. An Israel without a living connection with Diaspora Jewry, of which immigration is the most important expression, is a contradiction in terms. Just as Israel's past is inexplicable without this link, so is her future imponderable. If only for security reasons, though other factors are no less important, immigration is Israel's lifeblood.

ILLUSIONS

It would, of course, be an over-simplification to suggest that all the negative trends in Israel society are the result of governmental errors and blindness. The need to develop the economy at the dizzy tempo essential to provide a livelihood for tens of thousands of immigrants streaming into a poor country whose gates have never been closed; the weariness of veterans yearning for comfort and relaxation after years of sacrifice; the waves of hedonism which have engulfed youth all over the world in the shadow of threatening atomic destruction; the growing burden of security costs in face of Arab hostility—these and other factors would have placed even the most progressive government before objective difficulties which it would be folly to underestimate. There have been achievements as well as failures and it would be as unjustified to overlook the light as it is foolish to disregard the shadows.

The question is: now that the illusions fostered by *étatism* and capitalist normalisation are coming home to roost, will those who hold the sources of power wake up in time and draw the necessary conclusions from a bold analysis of their mistakes? For this is a question which determines the future not only of the kibbutz but of Israel as a whole.

WHITHER THE HISTADRUT?

One looks in vain to the mass organisation of the working class, the Histadrut, for signs of a change of heart. When the state is all-powerful, the Histadrut must accept a subordinate and dependent position. Perhaps the original sin can be traced back to the acquiescence of the Histadrut in the abolition of the independent workers' trend in education, whose schools catered for some 50 per cent of pre-State Israel's new generation, while the other half learned in general and religious schools.

With the introduction of state education, the workers' trend was abolished; yet the autonomous religious trend was maintained and increasingly dominates the education of the new generation. The Histadrut did away with its own schools in the name of "national unity"; yet it is clear that pre-State Israel was more united than post-State Israel, and the only result was that one of the most powerful instruments of the working class was needlessly sacrificed on the altar of state omnipotence, while clerical influence was permitted to grow and flourish.

This was a sign of things to come, The *Histadrut*, with its million members and serving 65 per cent of Israel's citizens, is larger and organisationally stronger than ever before. But it has become increasingly bureaucratic and divorced from the daily struggles of the worker. Its Mapai leadership has gradually whittled away its independence, for were such a powerful organisation to speak with a militant voice of its own, the whole conception of the state as "standing above sectional interests" would collapse.

It was easy enough for the Mapai majority to vote through such measures as the dissolution of the Palmach, the kibbutz-orientated striking force of the Haganah (voluntary pre-State defence-force); to do away with the *Histadrut* schools and ban for some years the work of the pioneering youth movements within the state schools. State affairs, it was explained, must be extricated from the political struggle.

But whose affair is it to revive the old pioneering spirit of the Haganah, to educate towards a life of labour on a border settlement, to induce the new generation to see its future far away from the bright lights of the city in the struggle against the desert? The State can build an army which is the pride of the nation and can count on the patriotism of citizen-soldiers in times of national emergency. But there is a grain of truth in the cynical statement that Israeli youth are prepared to die for the Negev but not to live in it.

Georges Friedmann points out (in his *End of the Jewish People?*) that

> once an "exploited social group" or "subject" nation has achieved its aim, social changes take place which are different from those for which the

revolutionaries prepared and hoped. Instead of the equality and fraternity of which they dreamed, the new liberty is accompanied by new social inequalities and group tensions . . . thus it is not incorrect to speak of a crisis of values in Israel society, particularly among the young. "The old dream has come true", a 50 year old engineer who emigrated from Rumania in 1950 said to me, "and nothing has taken its place".

VOLUNTARY IDEALISM

The fact is that the State is not all-powerful. The paraphernalia of the State is no substitute for personal belief in national and social ideals. It is becoming increasingly clear that if it is to be true to its own mission, Israel needs this voluntary idealism no less than it was needed in pre-State days. And if it was forthcoming then, it could be nurtured today far more effectively if the power and influence of the State, which dominates so many channels of public opinion and education, were directed to encouraging it.

But it cannot be achieved in a democratic state by orders, decrees and directives from the top, while down below social differentiation and careerism make a mockery out of the calls for pioneering, sacrifice and austerity voiced by public personalities on ceremonial occasions. New immigrants can be transported from the ships to development areas, but what is more understandable than that they will take their cue from the prevailing atmosphere of "I'm-all-right-Jack" as soon as they have passed through the first period of acclimatisation?

The capitalist can offer higher wages and other inducements to experts who would use their know-how in agricultural development areas or in the new mines and factories south of Beersheba, the capital of the Negev. But when the year, two-year or three-year contract expires, what is to stop the drift back to the comfort and conveniences of the metropolis? When pioneering physical labour and agriculture take second place in the scale of national values to more "respectable" occupations, it is inevitable that the immigrants will aim to follow in the footsteps of veterans who leave the field and factory for the higher pay and status of managerial work, commerce, offices and services in the cities.

State machinery can direct immigrants to new areas, but it cannot keep them there. The Jew is still drawn by strong magnets to urban concentrations, which grow and mushroom while the best available human resources are desperately needed far away in the development areas, in the countryside, on the borders. This is where the fate of the State of Israel will ultimately be resolved.

THE CRISIS OF VALUES AND THE WORKING CLASS

This is the background to what was called "the crisis of the kibbutz" in the 1950's. It is a part of a much deeper crisis of values which will determine the fate of Israel as a whole, and not only of the kibbutz. We have stressed that the criterion of kibbutz success cannot be measured only in its ability to provide a finer and juster way of life for its members, but no less in its role in the major processes of Zionist realisation and class struggle.

It will thrive in a progressive, pioneering and democratic regime, whose scale of values reflects the primacy of productive work, colonisation, working-class solidarity and independence. It will be tested by its ability to mobilise allies in the fight against anti-democratic and capitalist tendencies in which only the underprivileged will be forced into manual work while dog eats dog under the illiberal rule of a new aristocracy—the wealthy, the bureaucrats, the technocrats and Tammany-type political bosses.

These latter tendencies are most naturally expressed by the bourgeois parties, but the weakness and internal divisions of the Israeli bourgeoisie would not appear as yet to make it a serious candidate for power in the social and political reality of Israel. The real danger is that right-wing ideologies of liberalisation, free enterprise and capitalist normalisation, already largely accepted by some labour leaders as well as by the right-wing, will strengthen their foothold within the majority Labour party, and through it, within the *Histadrut* itself.

The social struggle in Israel differs from that in other newly independent states in one decisive aspect. There, the existing peasant and working-class forces must be organised and mobilised to develop the national economy and defend their class interests. *In Israel, these classes must be built as well as organised.* There they have behind them the inheritance of generations of labour, and the industrial proletariat has plentiful reserves among peasants who find a higher standard of living in urban industry than that to which they were accustomed in the countryside.

In Israel, the danger of "de-proletarisation" is ever present among first-generation workers and their children. The flow of immigration is unplanned, depending upon conditions in the Dispersion rather than those in Israel. Every new wave of immigration, particularly from under-developed countries, provides new reserves of unskilled labour, facilitiating the exit from the working class of more established workers into supervisory and managerial positions. There is a constant movement into the working class of those who have no alternative, and out of it for those who have learned the language, found their feet, and gained more experience of conditions in the new country. Today's worker is tomorrow's petit-bourgeois, and the working class lacks a solid core of rooted workers whose fate and fortune is permanently bound to that of their class and its social struggles.

The stabilisation of rooted and conscious industrial and agricultural working class is as much a national as a social need in Israel. Without it, the realisation of Zionism is inconceivable, just as the struggle for Socialism has no standard-bearer. The worker who dreams of flight from the working class has already deserted it in his consciousness. He hates work and envies his exploiter, whereas the conscious worker is proud of his labour and resents his exploiter. One will be happy that his son follows in his footsteps, while the other will do everything in his power to ensure that if not he, then at least his son, will leave the working class.

In the reality of Israel, only the kibbutz has crystallised a type of Jewish worker who guarantees the continuity from generation to generation of the tradition of labour and its political consciousness. There is no doubt this is one of the main contributions of the communal village to the whole of the young Jewish working-class movement. It explains why Mapai's kibbutz movement has always served as a catalyst for the more left-wing circles within that party, and why the Kibbutz Meuchad was forced out of Mapai and formed the nucleus of the more radical Socialist–Zionist Achdut–Avodah party.

In the most progressive, radical and militant Socialist–Zionist party, Mapam, the alliance between the kibbutz and the city worker is most highly developed and most consistently expressed. Its ideological platform represents the translation of the universal principles of Marxism to the special reality of the national and social struggle in Israel: the synthesis between pioneering Zionism and revolutionary Socialism, between national and class struggle.

It should also be noted that from its inception, Hashomer Hatzair has been the most militant and consistent protagonist of Jewish–Arab co-operation, solidarity and brotherhood. It rejects the conception that there is an unbridgeable contradiction between the historical interests of the two peoples, basing its Arab policy upon the conviction that genuine patriotism rests upon a synthesis of nationalism and internationalism, and fighting against every manifestation of chauvinism, Jewish as well as Arab.

Mapam, in which Arab citizens enjoy full and equal membership, led the struggle within the State of Israel for the abolition of the discriminatory Military Government in Arab areas, and fights for the granting of complete and equal civic, political, economic, social, educational and cultural rights for the Arab minority. The settlements of the Kibbutz Artzi play a leading role in the propagation of these ideas in neighbouring Arab villages, with which they have established close ties of friendship and mutual aid.

Within Mapam, both theory and practice are founded on the assumption that the historical interests of the commune and of the working class are inextricably woven together. This alliance is the rallying-point of the vanguard forces within the working class and the progressive intelligentsia. It binds together the struggles of the industrial worker for decent standards of living with those of the kibbutz which is the prototype of the future classless society and the strongest fortress of working class independence. In a sense, the class struggle in Israel depends upon the extent to which the city worker will come to the defence of the kibbutz and the kibbutz will be strong enough to defend the class interests of the city worker and his allies among the liberal professions, the artisans and the intelligentsia. In the long run, theirs is a common fate, and with both of them is determined the tempo of Zionist realisation and the advance towards Socialism.

If there is a "crisis" in the kibbutz, this is a reflection of the sharpening of the social struggle within Israel which accompanied the victorious conclusion of the struggle against a foreign power— a struggle in which social differences were naturally subordinated to the common interest of national independence. The battle against British rule was led by the young Jewish working-class and pioneering forces, whose constructive endeavours had already laid the basis for political independence before the British Mandate was finally terminated.

The state-in-the-making created a series of conditions which, with the winning of independence, could have paved the way to a rapid advance towards Socialism: the kibbutz movement, the political hegemony of the workers' parties within Israel and world Zionism, the economic power of the *Histadrut* and its industrial undertakings, progressive education, nationalised land, the co-operative movement in town and country, the Palmach, the secular and progressive character of the new Hebrew culture and the voluntary idealism and pioneering spirit of the cream of Israel's youth, inspired by great national and social ideals.

These and other corner-stones of Israeli society are for the most part connected directly or indirectly with the unique traditions of the Israeli Labour movement. They were founded on the Socialist–Zionist conception that the new Israel could only be built by a new type of Jew, one very different from the prototype of the Diaspora Jew. In order to take on flesh and blood, the principle of auto-emancipation demands an all-round revolution in Jewish life. Geographical concentration in Israel must be accompanied by the construction of a new society as well as a new land.

It was the Labour movement which set about this task, showing the way forward not only in the narrow political sense but as part of a broad conception of how to build the new society from rock-bottom, how to shape its very foundations. The whole of the *Histadrut*'s operation as a "State within a State" before 1948 (see p. 43) was motivated by the idea not only of defending the trade union interests of the workers but of actual independent working class creativity in all spheres, including a *Histadrut* economy of which the kibbutz and moshav were only one part.

Two decades after independence, these factors remain—in spite of all their manifest failings—the surest guarantee for the healthy development of the new Israeli economy and society. Was there any necessity for the gradual whittling away of these foundations in the 1950's and 1960's? Private capital would naturally build capitalist enterprise yet it is a fact that the great majority of the influx was of public capital. This was channelised into the artificial creation of a sector capitalist in ownership and operation yet built and backed to a large extent by national capital. On this basis one can readily understand the social changes, the changes of values, which inevitably accompanied the new direction. The purpose of Mapai, which set the pace in every government coalition since the State, seemed to be to replace the Socialist ideal with that of a welfare state, in which private and public enterprise would coexist but in which there would certainly be no preference for one sector over the other. Indeed, were Mapai to have had its way, some large, basic and profitable government concerns would have been sold into private hands.

We have dwelt on the trends in Israeli society because its capitalist orientation tended to emphasise the contradictions between the way of the kibbutz and that of the regime as a whole. We have noted that many progressive foundations have been subject to years of erosion. Yet it would be an unfounded oversimplification to imply that this erosion has undermined the foundations as such. Erosion is, in its very nature, a slow and gradual process. There can be no doubt that social, moral and spiritual phenomena unknown in former times have become commonplace: a decline in idealistic motivation among young people, unbridled egotism and selfishness, corruption in high and low places, the scramble for comfort and status seemingly at any price.

The economic crisis of the middle 1960's seemed to bring to light how deep a deterioration had set in and many saw the thousands of Israelis permanently leaving for other countries as a symbol of dangers which could become disasters.

There were those who hastened to draw the conclusion that bit by bit the whole fabric of Israeli society and of Zionism was coming apart.

THE SIX-DAY WAR

The prognosis of such prophets of gloom was upset, if not shattered, by the events of 5 to 11 June 1967. The Six-Day War, in which the Israel army defeated the combined forces of the Arab States in one of the shortest and most overwhelming armed victories of our times, was not only of profound political and military significance. (This is outside our scope here.) The Israeli soldiers who rose up against the openly declared Arab threat to destroy Israel once and for all, were part of a people's army. Few of them were professional soldiers yet they rallied as one man to the call and fought a war which in every conceivable sense of the words was won by the whole people. The comradeship in arms, heroism and readiness to sacrifice of the ordinary Israeli soldier almost surpasses description. This was the secret of the phenomenal military success.

This is, of course, incompatible with the picture of an Israeli society in an advanced state of disintegration. For such a cause, Israeli youth would not have been prepared or able to summon up such reserves of devotion. It is true that the question must be linked with the general atmosphere of a people which knows that it is fighting for actual survival against the threat of annihilation. However, any objective observer, even if writing too soon after the events to pretend to analyse them in depth, must draw the conclusion that the healthy foundations of Israeli national life proved their strength during the war. If the civilian-in-arms was ready to die for the young Jewish State, if the whole of the land and people (not to speak of world Jewry) demonstrated an overwhelming spirit of solidarity, this must surely indicate that the erosion of values about which we have spoken has not destroyed the mainstays of Israeli society. It may well indicate that it is not too late to reverse negative trends and launch a counter-attack designed to bolster the faith of Israelis in themselves and their future in times of peace as well as war.

The unforgettable days of June 1967 prove the basic validity of the Zionist conception of auto-emancipation. Removed by little more than two decades from the Nazi holocaust, they represent a unique historical contrast between a defenceless people, few of whom were capable of fighting back, and a free people ready and able to defend its newly won sovereignty. This ability and determination cannot be divorced from the achievements of Israel in building a new, modern and dynamic society. Within it, criticism of failures should not blind us to an appreciation of achievements. Both are an integral part of Israel's reality after twenty years and it is not by chance that the Six-Day War shattered conventional thinking, transforming the political scene and launching Israelis into a period of deep and far-reaching re-evaluations. A new generation is about to take over. The decisive question at stake is whether it will remain faithful to the general traditions of Labour-Zionism or will reject them as anachronisms. Once again it is superfluous to emphasise that these are issues in which the kibbutz, perhaps more than any other sector of Israeli life, is interested.

The war brought to the surface unexpected reserves of popular unity and belief in the common fate of the nation. The barriers dividing Israelis were lowered, revealing a people deeply and almost unanimously committed to the defence of their homeland. The hallmarks of the period were solidarity, mutual aid and the readiness of people to help each other. The border settlements, which for years had quietly, and often anonymously, born the brunt of Israel's security, became symbols of the embattled frontline, defended by the settlers in the name of the whole people.

It is no coincidence that the Commander-in-Chief of the Israel Army, Yitzchak Rabin, in a famous speech soon after the victory, made special mention of Nachal (the kibbutz-oriented army units which combine military training with agricultural settlement), and compared the present war to the heroic stand of kibbutzim like Negba in the War of Independence.* Both Rabin himself, and other army commanders whose achievements on various fronts amazed military experts all over the world, were raised in the tradition of the Palmach. There is a deep historical connection between the traditions of the Israel Labour movement and of the army. In daily conduct this is expressed in the army in the comradeship, the informality, the lack of snobbishness and of artificial distinctions between officers and men.

We have noted (see p. 139) that the younger generation from the kibbutzim plays a special role in the army. During the war this was tragically expressed in the casualty figures for 25 per cent of those who fell came from the kibbutzim, with their 3·8 per cent of the population. The kibbutz was able, through its very essence, to provide an example of complete mobilisation for every field of endeavour demanded by the war. Special mention should also be made of the volunteer movement from all over the world who came to help Israel in her hour of need in the summer of

---

* Rabin said that "war is intrinsically harsh and cruel and bloody, yet this war has brought forth rare and magnificent instances of heroism together with humane expressions of brotherhood, comradeship, and spiritual greatness. . . . The men in the front lines were witness not only to the glory of victory, but to the price of victory: their comrades who fell bleeding beside them. The terrible price which our enemies paid touched the hearts of many of our men as well. It may be that the Jewish people never learned and never accustomed itself to feel the triumph of conquest and victory and we receive it with mixed feelings. The Six-Day War revealed many instances of heroism far beyond the single attack which dashes unthinkingly forward. . . . Our warriors prevailed not by their weapons but by the consciousness of a mission, by a consciousness of righteousness, by a deep love for their homeland and an understanding of the difficult tasks imposed upon them: to ensure the existence of our people in its homeland, to protect, even at the price of their lives, the right of Israel to live in its own State, free, independent and peaceful."

1967; 4000 of the first 5000 volunteers were absorbed in the kibbutzim.

THE KIBBUTZ AND ITS ENVIRONMENT

The kibbutz is wide open to the influences of its surroundings: in this respect, it differs fundamentally from the relationship of Socialist to Capitalist countries. Though the internal economic structure and way of life of the kibbutz are socialistic, the relations of production between it and the national economy are capitalistic. The economic, social, cultural and ideological influences of the outside penetrate freely into the kibbutz. They undermine its self-confidence through emphasising its isolation, and belittle its internal sense of mission. At the same time, it becomes far harder for the kibbutz to mobilise, from within an environment hostile to its essence and apathetic to its fate, the manpower reserves it needs so badly.

Because it is part of a competitive society, the kibbutz must maintain its profitability, however serious its labour shortage. This is the background to the penetration into the kibbutz of hired labour —the most dangerous of the ways in which kibbutz values can be undermined under the pressure of its environment. Almost unconsciously, the manpower shortage forced some kibbutzim into a vicious circle from which it was unexpectedly hard to escape. They took on hired workers in order to fill a temporary gap, and found themselves unable to maintain the level of expansion and profitability thereby achieved, without this extra labour-force. Whatever its original justification, hired labour always proved easier to introduce than to eliminate.

Though there was a time when David Ben-Gurion publicly demanded that the kibbutz movement surrender the principle of self-labour as a "contribution" to the absorption of mass immigration, even those Mapai kibbutzim most influenced by his call gradually came round to the understanding that hired labour in productive and income-producing branches undermines the whole structure of the kibbutz. There is an unbridgeable gulf between the conception of the commune and that exploitation of outside workers which transforms the kibbutz member into a foreman and the kibbutz into an employer exploiting the labour of others, non-members, for profit.*

The kibbutz is, of course, entitled to the services of workers in building and other investments, or the work of a specially qualified expert from time to time, but we are referring to agricultural and industrial workers whose labour brings in direct profit to the kibbutz in the form of surplus-value. Those kibbutzim which went this way soon found that the same energy which the member showed as a worker he now invested in his job as a foreman. Some categories of the least desirable work could then become the monopoly of hired workers, whereas the kibbutz members would concentrate in more skilled jobs and administration.

The Kibbutz Artzi always saw hired labour as the Trojan horse of capitalism within the Socialist economy of the kibbutz so it has consistently stressed the principle of self-labour. Through careful manpower planning, increased mechanisation, ownership of a factory by more than one kibbutz, mutual aid to kibbutzim suffering from a particularly grave manpower shortage and the intervention wherever necessary of central movement institutions, the dimensions of hired labour in the K.A. have been greatly reduced. No new industry is permitted to be established unless it is based from the start on self-labour.

Between 1960 and 1965, hired labour in agriculture went down

---

* E. Kanovsky notes in his *Economy of the Israeli Kibbutz Movement* that "the problems which hired labour creates within the collective are manifold. The members who had at all times considered themselves as part and parcel of the 'working class' are now managers and 'exploiters'. One observer has noted that the exodus of members from kibbutzim is greatest in those settlements where hired labour is most prevalent. Others have noted that the second generation growing up in the collectives fails to see the difference between kibbutz life and other forms of social and economic organisation. What is probably worse is the lack of any job security which the hired labourers have, since they are aware of the fact that the collectives only employ them until they can replace them with one of their own members. . . ."

by 54 per cent and in industry by 35 per cent in the K.A. In 1966 hired labour in the K.A. accounted for 5·0 per cent of the labour force in agriculture and 13·7 per cent in industry, altogether 6 per cent of the labour force, 4·3 per cent excluding investments, building, etc. In the other kibbutz movements, the figures are less encouraging. In kibbutz industry as a whole, hired workers accounted for 59 per cent of the labour force in 1966.

THE INDISPENSABILITY OF THE KIBBUTZ

We have pointed to the increasing social differentiation which has developed during the years of statehood, but there are wide areas of activity in which interclass co-operation for common Zionist goals still serves the interests of the national bourgeoisie as well as those of the working class. This co-operation can, of course, be ended prematurely, but all classes are interested, even if for different reasons, in the upbuilding of the economy, the absorption of immigration, and the population and settlement of new areas. And because the kibbutz is irreplaceable as the pioneer of these processes, it enjoys a certain sympathy even among those who would prefer "kibbutzim without Socialism" as they put it.

This is to no small extent because of the role of the kibbutz in guarding Israel's security. Every border kibbutz is a stronghold ensuring the defence of the whole area around it. Remove the kibbutz, and the borders are wide open. Weaken the kibbutz and you strike a blow at Israel's security. Leave wide tracts unpopulated, and you invite armed infiltration into the heart of the country. Undermine security in outlying districts and you provide added impetus towards concentration in safer urban areas of new immigrants fearful for the security of their homes, their families and their children. The real borders are those of population, and the only land which is conquered for good is that which is worked and settled. In fact, the borders of the State of Israel as defined in 1949 are almost identical with the borders of kibbutz settlement, and it is only in the wake of the kibbutz that others settle and build their lives with a feeling of security and strength.

The pioneering stage in the building of Israel is far from over. This is best illustrated in the Negev, occupying over a half of Israel's land area, where it has scarcely begun. South of Beersheba, and with the exception of a few development towns rising out of the forbidding wasteland around, only isolated pioneer outposts challenge the endless miles of desert and wilderness still awaiting redemption.

Though private capital is interested, it will not take the risks involved in developing the Southern Negev, for even in easier conditions in the North it has been backed to the hilt by governmental concessions and safeguards.

The main burden will have to be accepted by national capital, which is already active in exploiting the chemical and other natural resources of the area. But in the prevailing atmosphere of careerism, who will pioneer this settlement? New immigrants sent straight from the ships will soon find their way back to the North. Only superior human material, from Jewish youth in Israel and abroad, sufficiently educated to utilise the findings of science and determined to stay put at all price and whatever the odds, has a chance of striking roots in this inhospitable environment.

A combination of industry, scientific research, the exploitation of local raw materials, transportation and tourism with agricultural experimentation and development—all these require a flexible form of settlement which must hold out in difficult security, as well as economic and social conditions. The kibbutz is uniquely adapted to undertake this mission and to do for the Negev what it has already achieved in areas in the North which once faced the same type of challenge. There is some reason to fear that unless a change of values comes in time, this challenge may remain unanswered and the rapid colonisation of the Negev—a dream.

We have tried to show how the cult of the state, the denigration of voluntary social forces and the processes of capitalist normalisation have thrown into relief the contradictions between the kibbutz and its environment.* Against the current trends, the kibbutz points to the superiority of a planned Socialist economy. It symbolises the continuity from generation to generation of a stable and conscious worker-farmer class, capable of managing its own affairs democratically and efficiently. It acts as a brake on the flight from the borders, the countryside and productive physical work, and typifies the merging of the ethnic groups into one united people as it absorbs pioneer youth from all over the world and ties their fate to that of its own second generation, deeply rooted in the soil and in the dignity of labour.

THE KIBBUTZ AND ITS ALLIES

Through decades of struggle and experience, the kibbutz has gained such qualitative and quantitative substance that its size and strength become independent factors of their own, with phenomenal powers of resistance to challenges which, had they come when the commune was small and weak, might have swept it into the archives of history. Neither does it stand alone, having proven its ability to mobilise powerful allies, most highly crystallised in Mapam but also exercising a strong influence in Achdut Avodah, Mapai (Labour party) and other progressive circles. What unites them is the understanding that there is no substitute for the kibbutz in the fulfilment of the national and social tasks for which the State of Israel was established, and that the stresses to which the kibbutz is subjected are symptoms of an attack upon the best elements in the new Israel.

This is one of the factors which has stimulated a new sense of common purpose in the various kibbutz movements. Joint econo-

---

* Georges Friedmann defines the four main trends hostile to the kibbutzim, which "sometimes mingle and re-inforce each other", as follows: "The first is indifference or hostility to Socialism . . . the second the disappointment caused by the course of development in the Soviet Union and the whiffs of anti-semitism from there, to which Hashomer Hatzair, which was very much oriented towards Soviet Communism, has been particularly sensitive." The third cause is "isolation" and the fourth "as a result, increasing recourse to paid labour".

mic enterprises have been established in order to serve all the local settlements—cotton gins, feed factories, plants for packing, storing and refrigeration, canning, poultry-processing, juices, etc. The purpose of these regional industries is to ensure that the agriculturalist will not be at the mercy of a private entrepreneur in order to prepare his produce for the market. (The American experience in this respect seems to show how easily the farmer may lose his economic independence.) The importance of this regional co-operation has grown in recent years as it has expanded in order to meet new needs in marketing, purchasing and financing as well as processing, and its value is no longer in question. What is under discussion nowadays is how to ensure that these large economic concerns are really controlled, as well as formally owned, by the settlements and how to diminish their dependence on hired labour. Another interesting question is where to fix the limits for this sort of enterprise and whether some functions, like the laundry, traditionally operated by the individual kibbutz, should be taken over by the region.

Joint consultation and representation between the Federations is already highly developed and the various movements are working more and more closely together on research into the economic and social problems of the kibbutz. In 1962 the Mapai kibbutzim returned to the joint teachers' training seminary which they had left some years previously. The overall organisation co-ordinating all forms of co-operation between the kibbutz movements, *Brith Hatnuah Hakibbutzit* (Union of the kibbutz movement), was founded in 1963. According to its constitution, only unanimous decisions are binding on the movements.

It is generally agreed that there is still enormous scope for increasing co-operation between the autonomous federations, to their mutual benefit. There are those who would like to go further and to transform the *Brith* into a complete union of the kibbutz movement, doing away with the existing divisions. It has usually been assumed that such a radical transformation can only come after the attainment of complete political and ideological unity between those Labour Zionist parties with which the kibbutz federations are associated. However, protagonists of kibbutz unity argue that overall labour unity could start in the kibbutzim and spread from them to the parties. The K.A., which has traditionally seen political unity as a condition of kibbutz unity, has lent all its efforts to strengthening the *Brith* on the assumption that whatever political developments are in store, deeper co-operation within the kibbutz movement can only benefit both the collectives and the whole Israel Labour movement.

It may be significant that though the Mapai and Achdut Avodah parties moved towards political unity in the middle 1960's, no suggestion was raised to unite the kibbutz movements associated with them. Only time can tell whether the great surge for unity which was so widely felt during the Six-Day War has a firm and lasting basis and can be translated into forms of genuine political unity.

A bitter harvest is being reaped by those who sowed the illusion that kibbutz values (such as the primacy and dignity of labour, social equality, grass-roots democracy, voluntarism and independent workers' management) have become anachronisms in the 1960's. Capitalist normalisation and state omnipotence have nurtured the spread of cynicism and the mistrust of any and every social ideal. This, along with the growth of bureaucracy, generates an atmosphere hardly calculated to buttress the mass immigration with idealistic elements which choose Israel as their home, and pioneering as their way of life, of their own free will. For if material comfort, easy living, and the bright lights of the city become criteria, Tel Aviv is a poor imitation of New York, London, or Paris.

The call for a return to the values best expressed in the kibbutz is not inspired by nostalgia for the past, but rather by an analysis of the present and an exploration of what the future holds in store for the new Israel. There is nothing new or forward-looking in the artificial attempts to fasten values transported from a different reality of highly developed capitalist economies and rich natural resources upon the growing body of Israel society.

This is the foundation for the belief that if the kibbutz will remain faithful to itself, the time will come when the failure of the new idols will become clear and the values of the commune will once again take their rightful place in the labour movement.

It would be idle to prophesy exactly how and when this change will come about, and in the ebb and flow of national and social struggle there may be disappointments, and even retreats, before the kibbutz will be able to break out of its enforced isolation and take its place at the head of Socialist forces which alone hold the answer to the dilemmas of modern society, in Israel as in the world.

TO WHOM DOES THE FUTURE BELONG?

This is a perspective strengthened by universal, as well as Israeli experience. Those who believe that capitalism has outlived its historical usefulness to mankind see national liberation as a stage on the road to social liberation under the leadership of progressive forces led by the working-class and inspired by faith in the ultimate victory of Socialism. These are the forces, among the Jewish people and the Zionist Movement, and within the working class struggling to establish itself in the special and exacting conditions of Israel's rebirth, of which the kibbutz is the vanguard and to which its future is inextricably bound.

The kibbutz, as we have stressed, was not built according to a blue-print. It could never have developed over a period of half a century as a stable way of life for over 80,000 men, women and children, embracing three generations, had it not increasingly thrown off the Utopian elements (which undoubtedly played a part in its initial stages) and anchored itself firmly in the great stream of history by which it was shaped and which it helped to shape. History never repeats itself exactly, so that it is doubtful whether it is more than an intellectual exercise to ask whether the unique combination of historical circumstances which facilitated its appearance and perpetuation can ever be re-created in the history of other lands and peoples.

Simone de Beauvoir summed her impressions and those of Jean-Paul Sartre after their visit to Israel and the kibbutzim in March

1967 during a visit to kibbutz Lehavot Habashan on the Syrian border:

> the kibbutzim had been described to us and they were called an authentic miracle. . . . I saw the kibbutz as it looks today, I saw the effort that you have put into it and the miracle which you have succeeded in achieving. I also saw a community of people that is different from all others which I have met until now. There is no exploitation or alienation within it and it lives with a sense of full equality and freedom. What you have accomplished can serve as an example to the world and I will conclude with the following wish: I hope that the world will follow your example.

The specific Israeli character of the kibbutz does not mean that it necessarily lacks elements of universal significance. Among the factors which substantiate the notion that the kibbutz is not entirely irrelevant to the wide world outside it, we may note: the post-Stalinist tendency in the Socialist world to move away from the monolithic conception that the construction of Soviet Socialism can serve as a universal model, and the recognition that there are different paths to Socialism according to the specific conditions in each country; the special and—as yet—unsolved problems encountered in the Socialist countries in their approach to the agrarian problem, and its overriding importance in many of the less developed newly-independent states of Africa and Asia; and the great dilemmas of modern mass-society—how to combine planning with freedom, overall centralisation with local democracy, and rational organisation at the top with personal initiative and identification at the bottom.

The kibbutz has never pretended to be a commodity for export. Even so, its own modest and restricted experience in agriculture, in the relationship of town and country, of manual to intellectual work, in human relations and incentives, democracy, equality and education—these may be of interest and importance to people in East and West, in more and less developed countries, who are searching for answers to the quandaries of our times in relation to the specific reality of their own national and social life.

These reflections may fortify the sense of pride in their achievements of those who devote their lives to building the kibbutz, and their consciousness of being a part of the forward surge of humanity towards a better world. Yet the salient fact remains that the major sense in which the kibbutz is, was and will always be for export is to be found in the challenge which it presents to progressive Jewish public opinion.

Above all, the vision of a new man and a new society personified in the kibbutz has always found its main response among Jewish youth all over the world. The same ideals which urged on the first bare-footed pioneers to bridge the gulf between the dream and its realisation in daily life are very much alive in the kibbutz as we know it today. The founders have aged, but not their ideal or the devotion which it seems capable of inspiring in future generations.

From this point of view the kibbutz movement represents a historical continuity for which there can be no substitute in Israel, for the Jewish people, or for Jewish youth everywhere. In this sense, the kibbutz is indeed irreplaceable because it is rooted in the deepest impulses both of Jewish and of all human history.

This is what Bialik, the poet laureate of the Hebrew revival, meant when he wrote: "only where there is a feeling that there is no way out is there utter devotion; and devotion is the touchstone of every truth in the world". Outside this context, one can neither understand the kibbutz nor fathom what sort of spiritual sustenance could nurture the sublime heroism of Mordechai Anielevich and his fighters in the doomed Warsaw ghetto.

Now, half a century after the birth of the kibbutz movement and twenty-five years after the ghetto revolt, both the ideal of the kibbutz and the demands which it imposes remain as dynamic and as stimulating as ever before. Individuals may rest on their laurels as they advance in age and stature, even in the age of tremendous social ferment and human accomplishment in which we live. Not so historical and revolutionary movements: for them history knows no respites—and least of all for those devoted to a cause as radical as the national and social renaissance of the Jewish people in its historical homeland.

That is why for the Kibbutz Artzi, the achievements of the past are no more than foundations, moulded and tested through decades of experience to face the challenge of the future, with all the hazards, and all the promise, which it holds out.

Bibliography

THE following bibliography does not pretend to be comprehensive but rather to list the more important books in English about the kibbutz.

The Other Society, by Dr. H. DARIN-DRABKIN (Victor Gollancz, London, 1962).

Patterns of Cooperative Agriculture in Israel, by Dr. H. DARIN-DRABKIN (Dept. for International Assoc. for Rural Planning, Israel Institute for Books, Tel-Aviv, 1962).

The Purest Democracy in the World, by ABRAHAM C. BEN-YOSEF (Herzl Press and Thomas Yoseloff, New York–London, 1963).

Life in a Kibbutz, by MURRAY WEINGARTEN (Reconstructionist Press, New York, 1955).

Kibbutz, Venture in Utopia, by E. MELFORD SPIRO (Harvard Univ. Press, Cambridge, Mass., 1958).

Children of the Kibbutz, by E. MELFORD SPIRO (Harvard Univ. Press, Cambridge, Mass., 1958).

The End of the Jewish People?, by GEORGES FRIEDMANN (Hutchinson, London, 1967).

The Economy of the Israeli Kibbutz, by ELIYAHU KANOVSKY (Harvard Univ. Press, 1966).

A History of the Cooperative Movement in Israel, Book 2: *The Evolution of the Kibbutz Movement*, by HARRY VITELES (Valentine Mitchell, 1967) *and Book 3*.

The Kibbutz that Was, by BORIS STEIN (Public Affairs Press, Washington, 1965).

Agricultural Planning and Village Community in Israel, edited by J. BEN-DAVID (UNESCO, 1964).

Growing Up in the Kibbutz, by A. I. RABIN (Springer, New York, 1965).

Bibliography of the Kibbutz, by E. COHEN, Givat Chaviva, Israel.

Statistical Appendix:
The Kibbutz in Figures

TABLE 1. THE KIBBUTZ POPULATION, 30 SEPTEMBER 1967

Federation	Political affiliation	Number of Kibbutzim	Population	Per cent
Whole kibbutz movement		225	93,210	100
Kibbutz Artzi Hashomer Hatzair	Mapam	73	32,061	34·5
Ichud Hakvutzot V'hakibbutzim	Mapai★	75	28,936	30·4
Hakibbutz Hameuchad	Achdut Ha'avodah★	57	25,609	27·7
Hakibbutz Hadati	National Religious Party (Poale Mizrachi)	10	3,987	4·2
Haoved Hatzioni†	Independent Liberals	5	1,300	1·7
Poalei Agudat Yisrael	Poalei Agudat Yisrael	2	448	0·7
Others	Unaffiliated	3	869	1·0

★ Since 1968 part of the Israel Labour party.

† Organizationally linked with the *Ichud* federation.

Source: The Audit Union of Workers' Agricultural Co-operative Societies.

Note: Government statistics differ somewhat from those of the Audit Union and recorded a population of 83,310 in 233 kibbutzim on 31 Dec. 1967. This is due not only to the different census date but also to the different criteria adopted as regards categories of population and settlements to be included in the figures. The figures of the Statistical Department of the Kibbutz Artzi also show slight variations for similar reasons.

TABLE 2. THE KIBBUTZ MOVEMENT AND THE JEWISH POPULATION OF ISRAEL

Date	Jewish population	Kibbutz population	Percentage
1 Oct. 1930	175,000	4,506	2·57
1 Oct. 1934	307,700	7,521	2·47
1 Oct. 1935	375,400	12,500	3·33
1 Oct. 1936	404,400	15,500	3·83
1 Oct. 1937	417,200	16,500	3·98
1 Oct. 1938	436,700	18,200	4·17
1 Oct. 1939	474,600	22,600	4·76
1 Oct. 1940	492,400	25,900	5·24
1 Oct. 1941	504,600	26,000	5·15
1 Oct. 1942	517,200	26,000	5·03
1 Oct. 1943	539,000	31,200	5·79
1 Oct. 1944	565,000	35,300	6·25
1 Oct. 1945	592,000	37,400	6·32
1 Oct. 1946	625,000	43,595	6·97
1 Oct. 1947	649,000	47,408	7·30
8 Nov. 1948	758,700	54,221	7·15
1 Oct. 1949	963,000	63,518	6·60
1 Oct. 1950	1,152,000	64,029	5·56
1 Oct. 1951	1,383,000	67,618	4·89
1 Oct. 1952	1,441,000	69,991	4·86
1 Oct. 1953	1,483,000	71,569	4·83
1 Oct. 1954	1,518,000	74,558	4·91
1 Oct. 1955	1,580,000	80,348	5·09
1 Oct. 1956	1,655,000	81,213	4·90
1 Oct. 1957	1,747,000	83,942	4·80
1 Oct. 1958	1,802,000	83,073	4·51
1 Oct. 1959	1,851,000	81,946	4·43
1 Oct. 1960	1,902,000	80,155	4·21
1 Oct. 1961	1,970,000	81,380	4·13
1 Oct. 1962	2,054,000	82,467	4·01
1 Oct. 1963	2,133,800	85,051	3·98
1 Oct. 1964	2,219,000	85,818	3·87
1 Oct. 1965	2,284,300	87,162	3·82
1 Oct. 1966	2,334,000	88,402	3·79
1 Oct. 1967	2,372,000	93,210	3·93

Source : The Audit Union; The Government Year Book.

TABLE 3. POPULATION GROWTH IN THE KIBBUTZ ARTZI, 1927–67

Year	Kibbutzim	Members and candidates	Kibbutz children	Youth Aliya and outside children	Parents	Others	Total Population
1927	4	250					
1939	24	5007	927	320	88	95	6437
1942	39	5561	1665	239	123	112	7790
1945	40	6249	2896	972	167	168	10,452
1946	44	7222	3304	1406	217	172	12,401
1947	49	7898	3878	1651	260	297	13,984
1948	52	9543	4485	1882	342	210	16,462
1949	61	10,206	4894	3380	450	205	19,135
1950	65	10,671	5481	3126	613	279	20,170
1951	66	11,198	6082	3642	668	326	21,916
1952	67	11,260	6692	3526	691	248	22,417
1953	68	11,956	7274	3388	719	253	23,590
1954	68	12,800	7797	3254	772	425	25,084
1955	70	13,499	8336	3082	809	323	26,049
1956	72	13,656	8644	2947	865	371	26,483
1957	73	13,880	8946	3006	957	873	27,662
1958	73	14,336	9163	2589	936	642	27,666
1959	73	14,134	9354	2543	940	662	27,633
1960	73	14,089	9445	2228	934	610	27,306
1961	73	14,167	9429	2221	930	672	27,419
1962	73	14,345	9469	2124	903	822	27,663
1963	73	15,069	9468	2104	925	909	28,475
1964	73	15,777	9430	1713	910	919	28,749
1965	73	16,326	9465	1462	907	1054	29,214
1966	73	16,879	9357	1386	889	953	29,464
1967	73	17,562	9447	1179	878	1152	30,218

Source: Statistical Department of the Kibbutz Artzi.

TABLE 4. COMPOSITION OF KIBBUTZ ARTZI, 1966

Category	Percentage
Members and candidates	57·2
Kibbutz children	32·0
Youth Aliya	2·8
Outside children	1·9
Parents of members	2·9
Others	3·2

Source : Statistical Department of the Kibbutz
Artzi.

TABLE 5. KIBBUTZIM OF THE K.A.
ACCORDING TO THE NUMBER OF
SOULS, 1966

Number of souls	Kibbutzim
Above 700	2
Above 600	7
500–600	16
400–500	13
300–400	11
200–300	14
100–200	7
Up to 100	3

Source : Statistical Department of the
Kibbutz Artzi.

TABLE 6. THE DEVELOPMENT AND STRUCTURE OF THE POPULATION
IN A VETERAN KIBBUTZ—MISHMAR HAEMEK

Mishmar Haemek, the second kibbutz of the K.A., was founded in 1922 and settled on the land in 1926. The following figures show the growth of its population from 1922 to the end of 1965

A. *Population growth*

Year	Members	Candidates	Temporary population	Youth Aliya	Kibbutz children	Outside children	Members' parents	Total
1922	81	—	—	—	—	—	—	81
1930	93	—	—	—	19	—	—	112
1935	102	—	29	20	50	—	19	220
1940	130	—	58	—	86	35	14	323
1945	183	3	29	23	119	20	15	392
1950	235	5	52	43	140	109	20	604
1955	308	26	6	18	153	9	32	552
1960	336	55	24	—	199	12	34	660
1961	344	53	38	29	203	—	33	707
1965	349	60	72	—	241	11	26	769

B. *The older and younger generations*

Breaking down the kibbutz *membership* (excluding children, older parents, etc.), we find the following division in 1965:

Age 60 and over	85 members
Age 50 to 59	50 members
Age 30 to 49	154 members
Age 20 to 29	60 members
Candidates	60

We can also divide the membership into younger and older generations. The older generation is composed of founder-members and those who joined up to 1940 along with a few older people who joined later on. The younger generation is composed of sons of the kibbutz who were accepted as members from the year 1940, and graduates of the kibbutz high school, of Youth Aliya, and of the Israeli Hashomer Hatzair, all of whom were accepted as members since 1940. The division between the generations is as follows:

Older generation   135 members, 39·5 per cent

Younger generation   214 members, 60·5 per cent

These significant figures provide a key to an understanding of the healthy and organic process of growth in the kibbutz: over the years, 135 members of the older generation succeeded in "absorbing" 214 members of the younger generation.

C. *Who stayed and who left?*

Of the founder-members, only fifteen left the kibbutz between 1927 and 1962 (17 per cent), and only three (3·4 per cent) during the last twenty-eight years.

Over a period of twenty-one years, ninety sons and daughters joined the kibbutz as members. Of these ninety, seventeen (19·9 per cent) left Mishmar Haemek, but of these nine joined other kibbutzim. In fact, only three gave up kibbutz life of their own free decision.

TABLE 7. THE FOUNDING KIBBUTZIM OF K.A. AFTER 40 YEARS (1927–67)

Kibbutz	1927			1967		
	Members	Children	Total population	Members	Children	Total population
Mishmar Haemek	82	18	100	379	254	750
Ma'abarot	34	—	34	290	166	590
Hertzlia (Merchavia)	56	3	59	276	164	585
Ein Ganim[1] (Ein Shemer)	51	1	52	259	150	589
K.A. Section of Beth Alpha	9	—	9	383	223	667
Bivracha[2] (Sarid)	31	1	32	325	179	681

[1] United with Kibbutz Brenner, Karkur.

[2] Joined K.A. in 1930.

Source: Statistical Department of the Kibbutz Artzi.

KIBBUTZ ARTZI HASHOMER HATZAIR IN 1967
KIBBUTZIM AND DATES OF SETTLEMENT

Amir (1939)
Baram (1949)
Barkai (1949)
Beit Alfa (1922)
Beit Nir (1957)
Beit Kama (1949)
Beit Zera (1926)
Carmia (1950)
Dalia (1939)
Dan (1939)
Dvir (1951)
Ein Dor (1948)
Ein Hachoresh (1931)
Ein Hamifratz (1938)
Ein Hashofet (1937)
Ein Shemer (1927)
Eilon (1938)
Evron (1945)
Gaash (1951)
Gaaton (1948)
Galon (1946)
Gan Shmuel (1920)
Gat (1941)
Gazit (1948)
Givat Oz (1949)
Gvulot (1944)

Hachorshim (1955)
Haogen (1947)
Hamaapil (1945)
Harel (1948)
Hatzor (1946)
Hazorea (1936)
Idmit (1958)
Kfar Masaryk (1938)
Kfar Menachem (1939)
Lahav (1952)
Lehavot Habashan
  (1945)
Lehavot Chaviva (1949)
Maabarot (1933)
Maanit (1942)
Magen (1949)
Megiddo (1949)
Merchavia (1926)
Mesillot (1938)
Metzer (1953)
Mishmar Haemek
  (1926)
Mizra (1924)
Nachshon (1950)
Nachshonim (1949)
Negba (1939)

Nir David (Tel Amal)
  (1936)
Nirim (1949)
Nir Oz (1955)
Nir Yitzchak (1949)
Ramat Hashofet (1940)
Ramot Menashe (1948)
Revadim (1948)
Reshafim (1948)
Ruchama (1944)
Saar (1948)
Sarid (1926)
Sasa (1949)
Sdeh Yoav (1957)
Shaar Ha'amakim (1935)
Shaar Hagolan (1937)
Shamir (1944)
Shomrat (1948)
Shuval (1946)
Yad Mordechai (1943)
Yakum (1947)
Yasur (1949)
Yechiam (1946)
Zikim (1949)

DATE DUE

AUG 4 '70	NOV 22 '74		
OCT 21 '70	DEC 6 '14		
JAN 9 '71	JAN 7 '76		
MAY 4 '71	Jan 22 76		
DEC 17 '71	NOV 18 '76		
JAN 7 '72	DEC 6 '76		
APR 17 '72	DEC 21 '76		
MAY 1 '72	DEC 6 '76		
NOV 8 '72	MAY 13 '81		
DEC 11 '72	APR 15 '83		
JAN 3 '73			
APR 13 '73			
MAY 4 '73			
MAY 16 '73			
OCT 10 '73			
DEC 3 '73			
APR 19 '74			
OCT 2 '74			
GAYLORD			PRINTED IN U.S.A.